EVERY DECISION
MATTERS

ARNOLD L. HARVEY II

EVERY DECISION MATTERS

Our Decisions Will Determine Our Destiny

YorkshirePublishing
www.yorkshirepublishing.com
Write Now.

ISBN: 978-1-947825-31-4
Every Decision Matters
Copyright © 2013 by Arnold L. Harvey II

Yorkshire Publishing
3207 South Norwood Avenue
Tulsa, Oklahoma 74135
www.YorkshirePublishing.com
918.394.2665

CONTENTS

INTRODUCTION

It is not what happens to us in life that matters. It is
how we *decide* to react.

For the longest time, I tried to make sense of all the hell
I went through in my life. It just did not seem fair to
me that my life was destroyed by the hands of someone else.
The hurt and pain I experienced physically, emotionally, and
mentally were unbearable. The nightmares haunted me in my
sleep. The justice system failed me. My wife and child left me.
Had God forsaken me? Finally, I came to my breaking point.
I did not want to go on living. *I might as well just end it now*
was the predominant thought running through my mind. In a
drunken rage, I finally cried out for God to either put me out
of my misery or to help me.

Then suddenly something changed in me. My life was
spared. I unknowingly made a *decision* that night that would
forever change my life. My life began to be completely restored
and renewed. I tapped into a power that was previously
unknown to me.

Throughout all of this, I found out how important each and every *decision* I made was. I learned that our destiny is ultimately shaped by our *decisions*. Life is going to knock us down and beat us up from time to time. The key is that it does not matter how many times we end up flat on our back. It only matters how many times we *decide* to get up and continue to fight.

TRAGEDY

S team rose from the dark rivers of crimson flowing in the frigid German air. I lay there in the dark on the frozen asphalt, fighting for my life. Blood poured like waterfalls from the gaping wounds on my face, arm, and back. I couldn't feel my legs, and my lungs filled with blood, making it almost impossible to breathe. My body began to shiver violently from the massive loss of blood coupled with the temperature being in the low teens. This was it! This was how it was all going to end! Fear of the unknown terrified me. Thoughts of my unborn child never knowing her father flashed through my mind. Visions of my mother crying over my casket as they slowly began lowering it in the ground haunted me.

"Hold on, Arnold, you have to fight!" Sean yelled to me. "Don't die, your daughter needs you. Think about Theresa, hold on for her." Sean knelt behind me, propping me up into the seated position.

The blood filling my lungs made it difficult to speak, but I was able to reply, "I'm so scared. I don't think I am going to make it. Please take care of my baby for me, and tell my family I love them."

"You're going to tell them yourself because you are going to pull through this," Sean said through the tears.

The sounds of the gasps and screams from the onlookers echoed in my ears. I could see people all around me; there was so much commotion and noise from the horrified crowd that it was overwhelming. Panic, anxiety, and fear ravaged my mind. Thoughts were moving at the speed of light. I saw images of the people that I loved. I saw the grieved looks on their faces when they found out I had died. The only thing I could think to do was to start praying to God. Before this time, I never had a really good relationship with God. I was not sure if he even existed, but if he did, he was the only one who could save me.

In an instant, everything changed. In the blink of an eye, there was absolute silence. I could see the people around me, but there was no sound at all. The light from the streetlamp above grew soft and warm. The fear and worry that gripped me like a vise was gone. As I lay motionless on the frozen ground, the pain from the wounds was taken away. Silent, warm, comfortable I felt as though I had entered into a warm bath. The most overwhelming feeling of love engulfed my entire being. This feeling of love was more powerful than every feeling I had ever felt up until that point combined. I literally experienced the presence of God. He wrapped me in his arms; the essence of him engulfed my entire being. There was a peace that cannot be explained in words. I embraced him with all of my heart in that moment and knew that whether I lived or died his will would ultimately be done. I finally submitted to God for the first time in my life. All my life I did what I wanted to do. I never allowed him to be in control. I thought I could handle everything. This of course was different. I finally had the answer to the question I had been asking my entire life, which was *Does he really exist?*

My eyelids began to feel extremely heavy, so heavy that it was impossible to keep them open. I wanted to sleep, I was just so tired. The feelings of comfort and love cradled me and were slowly rocking me to sleep. I could no longer fight the feeling any longer, and I finally surrendered to the slumber.

Beep, beep, beep, beep was the first noise I heard. I began to peer through the thin opening in my eyelids. The beeping continued while the thin opening widened ever so slowly. It was hard to make anything out around me; my vision was extremely blurry. I was finally able to open my eyes completely, and I blinked them several times in attempt to focus my vision. After a few seconds, I was able to make out my surroundings. Above me all, I could see were fluorescent lights in the ceiling. I knew I was in some sort of room, but I wasn't sure where or why. The constant beeping behind me sounded like the machines I had heard before in hospitals, but why? I tried to move my arms, but they were restrained to the bed. I tried to speak, but I couldn't because there was a large tube going down my throat. What on earth was going on here? I must have been in some sort of dream.

Oh my God, I thought. *I can't move my legs.* Panic set in, and the beeping of the machines behind me started to pick up the pace,. *This is a nightmare. I am in a horrible nightmare. I am asleep, and I need to wake up* were the thoughts that raced through my head. I began to try and shake myself awake, but as I moved, severe pain pierced through my upper body. *Please, God, tell me what is going on?* I pleaded in my mind. *I am so scared, where am I and what happened to me?*

Just then, the door swung open, and my wife burst into the room. She was eight months pregnant with our daughter, and I could see the pain in her eyes. She rushed over to my side and gently touched my head.

"Arnold, sweetie, this is not a dream," she said with tears streaming down her face. "You and Sean were stabbed four days ago. Sean is okay, but you have a very serious injury, baby."

I looked up at her in shock. The tube in my throat prevented me from asking any of the million questions that raced through my mind.

"I have to tell you this, and I don't know how to say it to you," she said, wiping her tears from her eyes. "One of the stab wounds hit your spinal cord. The doctors think that you may never be able to walk again."

Oh my God, no, please, God, no, I thought. This was too much to take in. I couldn't process all this information. My mind was on overload. I still couldn't understand how this happened.

Just then, the door swung open again. In rushed two men in long white coats. They came in the room speaking German to each other. They stood next to my wife, and they all three began having a conversation in German. Luckily, my wife was a Romanian gypsy; she was raised in Germany, so she spoke it fluently. The three spoke for what seemed like an eternity. The whole time, I was lying there, not understanding a word that they were saying.

What in the hell happened to me? I thought. While they were talking, I was trying my hardest to remember what had happened. All of a sudden, a flash of Sean getting stabbed in his back flashed through my mind. It was like I took a picture with my mind. In the image, I saw many people around Sean and me; it was dark in the image, so it had to be at night. There was a guy holding a knife and driving the tip of the knife into Sean's upper back. Just then, another imaged flashed in my mind of me rushing toward the man with the knife, and him turning the knife toward me.

The doctor to the right of my wife cut in. "Mr. Harvey, we are going to take the tube from your throat now." He had an extremely thick German accent that made it hard to make out what he said. He reached down and slowly pulled the tube that was down my throat out of my mouth. I could feel it moving from deep within. I felt like I was choking, and my throat began contracting around the plastic. The end of the long tube finally reached my mouth, and it was finally out. Even though the tube was already out, I still could not speak.

My breathing was very weak, and it was hard to get air in and out of my lungs.

My wife spoke again. "Baby, I am going to translate what the doctors are saying." The man to the left of her said a long sentence in German. "The doctor says he is the doctor that was here when you came to the hospital the other night." The doctor continued. "He says that you are very blessed to be alive. He says that there were a total of twelve stab wounds in your body, and when you got to the hospital, you had already been pronounced dead once in the ambulance. The paramedics were able to revive you, but you were barely alive when they got you to the emergency room. They immediately had to take you into surgery because your lung had collapsed and was completely filled with blood. They opened you up and had to remove a portion of your lung and insert three tubes to drain the blood."

I looked down to my right side and saw the tubes protruding from me. *This can't be real,* I thought. *I can't believe this happened to me. I can't believe that this is real.* I still could not come to grips with the fact that this was real life. It still seemed like it was a dream and I was going to wake up any minute and be lying in my bed unharmed. I just wanted to wake up and be okay.

My wife continued translating. "The doctor says that during the surgery, they had to do emergency CPR and shock you with the paddles because your heart stopped beating again. They luckily were able to revive you, and they completed the surgery successfully. During all of this, you used up their entire supply of A positive blood type for the entire area. They had to transfuse forty-eight pints of blood into your body. He says that the human body only holds twelve, so you are now officially German because your blood has been completely replaced four times over with German blood," she said with a very weak chuckle. "He also says that there was one more scare with you in ICU. The emergency response team had to come in and shock you again because your heart stopped for the third time."

The doctor to the right of my wife cut in. "Mr. Harvey, you must be a cat because you have used up three of your nine lives."

An image of the incident flashed through my mind as the doctor said that. I saw my assailant driving the knife into my left arm. I remembered the pain; I felt the knife plunge into me. It was the worst pain I had ever felt in my life. The image switched to a short memory of the knife being lodged in my arm and the person attacking me trying to pull it out. The pain was unbearable. I switched my focus to my left arm and tried to move it. A sharp, deep internal pain throbbed within my left bicep. My thoughts then switched back to the assault. There were so many people all around me and there were punches being thrown from every direction. The assailant finally got the knife out of my arm, and I remembered grabbing my left bicep where the massive wound was. I remembered the sharp pain that went so deep into my arm. I looked up and saw him wield the knife again at me, striking just above my left eyebrow, and slicing downward just above my left eye. I saw the blood running down into my eye. The pain from the new wound above my eye distracted me from the gaping hole in my arm.

My wife interrupted the memory by saying, "Baby, are you, okay?" She could see that I had drifted off into deep thought. "Blink your eyes if you're okay for me to continue."

I blinked my eyes twice, signaling to her that she was able to go on.

"The doctor says that they don't believe that you will be able to walk ever again, sweetie," she said softly. "He says that the knife went into your back and severed a portion of your spinal cord. The spinal cord does not regenerate, honey."

I was crushed inside as she said those words. *How could this be?* I thought. My attention went to my legs. I could see them under the blanket, but it felt as if they weren't there. I tried to move them. I couldn't feel or move anything. More sadness flooded into my being. I had the feeling of complete hopelessness.

My mind then drifted back into the memory of my attack. The vision picked up with me rushing forward to grab my attacker. I remembered thinking, *I have no choice but to rush him and try to take the knife.* I wrapped him up with the tightest bear hug I could manage in hope of getting him on the ground. I knew if I got him on the ground, I could overpower him and get the knife away. But as we grappled, he reached around me with the knife still in his right hand and plunged the tip into my back. As soon as the knife went in, I lost all feeling from my chest down and collapsed. I was defenseless on the ground. I remembered how terrified I was during all this. While I was lying facedown on the cold ground, motionless and scared, I felt the horrible pain of the eight-inch serrated piece of steal entering my body again. The knife went so deep into my back that I could feel it in my core. Then the steel savagely entered my body again, then again, and again, and again. He stabbed me ten more times while I was completely helpless and motionless. I couldn't bear to think about it anymore.

"There is hope though," my wife interrupted my thought once more. "The doctors said they believe that the knife only severed the spinal cord halfway. So there is a very small chance that you may be able to walk again. He says that they predict that there is maybe a 10 percent chance that you will regain some feeling, and be able to walk."

My mind immediately went to the worst-case scenario. I pictured myself in a wheelchair, unable to feel anything. I felt the weight of the sadness upon me. It felt like an elephant was sitting on my chest. A tear streamed down my cheek. *My life is over,* I thought. I just had my twenty-first birthday two months ago. I was in the best shape of my life. Now I am going to be in a wheelchair forever. I am expecting my first child in a month. What good will I be to her? I closed my eyes and began to cry.

My wife wrapped her hands around my head, and we cried together. We were both scared about how the future would be. We knew that our lives would never be the same again.

DECISION

The doctors left the room, and my wife and I sat alone quietly. The silence was interrupted by my wife groaning.

"Owww, I think I just felt a contraction," she said. We sat quietly again for several minutes to see if there would be another one. "I think I feel one coming! Oh my goodness, owwww! Please, God, no, don't let me go into labor now!" she pleaded.

There was nothing I could do; I felt helpless. Here was my wife, starting to go into labor, and I could do absolutely nothing.

Her breathing started to quicken. "Here comes another one!" She let out another loud moan. "I am going to push the button and call the doctors in." She pushed the emergency button, and an alarm started to sound. Two nurses came rushing in and started speaking in German with her.

Again, I was lying there, too weak to move and not able to understand what they were talking about. By this time, the nurses had already removed the restraints from my hands, so I picked my right arm up and stretched it toward her. She grabbed my hand and squeezed it.

"Baby, they think I may be going into labor. They are going to take me to the labor and delivery section of the hospital," she said with a sense of fear in her voice.

One of the nurses left the room and returned quickly with a wheelchair for my wife. They helped raise her up and set her down gently into the chair.

"Everything's going to be okay, honey," she said. "Don't worry. Try and get some rest. You need your strength. They are going to take care of you while I'm gone."

They left with her, and I was alone in the room. I tried my hardest to calm down because the tension was causing my wounds to hurt even worse. *Is it possible that it can get any worse than this?* I thought to myself. *My first child may come, and I am going to miss the birth because I am lying here, paralyzed.* This was way too much for me to handle. The stress inside consumed me. I became so tired. All I could think about was going to sleep. I didn't want to face this horrific reality I was going through. I closed my eyes and went to sleep.

I awoke to the sound of a familiar voice. "Hello, my son, how are you feeling?" The voice was my mother's, but how was that possible?

I opened my eyes, and there stood, my mother. She looked like she hadn't slept in several days. Her eyes were swollen, and I could tell she had been crying a lot. *How on earth…?* I thought to myself. I was lying in a German hospital, looking at my mother whom I hadn't seen in almost a year.

Again, she spoke. "Hello, my son, it's me, Mom." She grabbed my hand and started to rub my head gently. "I tried to get here as soon as I could, but I didn't have a passport. God is so good though because he opened doors for me that no person could have possibly opened. As soon as I got to the passport office on Monday, I had my passport the next day, it was nothing short of a miracle!" she exclaimed.

A wonderful feeling came over me. My mother and I have always been close. I'm what you might call a momma's boy. She and I have been through a lot together. No matter what, she was always there for me in every situation. So seeing her there was definitely a relief; the weight of the world that was on my chest was lightened by her strength.

I tried to speak again and was able to make out a couple words. "Hi, Ma." My voice was like a whisper.

"You don't have to speak," she said softly. "I am going to take care of you now." My mother was a nurse's aid for many years when I was growing up. She was used to working with very sick people, and her old training just kicked right in.

Suddenly, my mind shifted to my wife. *Is she okay?* I thought. *Did she have the baby? Is the baby okay?* I gathered my strength to speak again. "Where is Tracy?"

"The doctor tried to explain to me the best he could that she was stable," my mother replied. "He said that she ended up not going into full labor. They were able to stop it, but the stress she has been going through has really been hard on her and the baby."

Whhheeeww! Was my first thought. I was so relieved; that was one less thing that I had to be stressed out over. A nurse wheeled Tracy in the next morning, and we all three hugged.

Several days went by, and my mother and Tracy helped so much with taking care of me. The only problem was, it took a little while getting used to my mother changing my diapers. As each day passed, I gained a little more strength, and eventually I was able to talk again. However, people had to do basically everything for me. I had to be fed, changed, and rolled from side to side. I felt like I was starting all over from a baby again. Although I was going through all this, the initial depression was beginning to wear off. I was in pretty good spirits because of the fact I was alive. It was made very clear to me by my mother that I should be *grateful* for the fact that I will get to see my family and raise my new baby girl. I started looking at life in a different way once I started being *grateful* for what I had instead of being bitter for what I didn't have.

Very often, different doctors would come in and speak to my wife, and she would translate for them. We started working on strengthening my lungs with this weird little device I had to blow in, but it worked. There was also a physical therapist that started to visit me in the mornings. We started working on sitting up. The first time I sat up, I felt like I was about to throw up. It made me so dizzy and nauseated that I had to lie back down immediately. My physical therapist also tried to get me to concentrate on moving my legs. We would do exercises where all I would be doing was staring at my feet and trying to wiggle my toes. Each time I tried, there was no movement at all. It began to get pretty frustrating not being able to move them, and I was starting to give up hope already for walking again.

One evening, a man that I had never seen before came into my room. He was very nicely dressed in a dark suit. He was completely bald and had sunglasses propped up on the top of his head. He was also carrying a dark briefcase. I was shocked to see him; he didn't look like anyone else who had come into my room since I had been here. As he walked toward my bedside, I could see the badge hanging around his neck.

"Hello, Mr. Harvey," the man said. "My name is Detective Thomas. I am here to discuss what happened to you the other night." He stuck his hand out for me to shake. I pulled my hand from under the blanket and gave him the firmest handshake I possibly could. "Wow, you are a fighter, aren't you, Mr. Harvey?" he said. "I am glad to see that you are getting your strength back already." He pulled up a chair from the other side of the room and sat down beside me. "Now first of all, I want to let you know that we have been working on this case tirelessly. My team of investigators and I have taken a serious interest in this case due to the level of brutality demonstrated. We have several suspects, but we have had very conflicting eyewitness accounts of what took place. The majority of the people that were there admitted to being extremely intoxicated and were involved in the huge brawl themselves. I need to know from you if you think you can identify the man who stabbed you?"

I had tried not to think about the incident as much as I could up until this point. But I knew that I was going to have to visit the painful memories sooner or later. My mind went to an image of my attacker facing me with the knife. I could see his face clearly; it was vividly etched in my mind.

"Yes, sir," I said. "I will be able to point him out with 100 percent certainty," I assured him.

"That is exactly what I wanted to hear from you, Mr. Harvey," Detective Thomas replied. "Now my team and I have narrowed it down to about ten people that may have done this or were at least involved on some level. I have my suspicions of whom it may be, I just need you to point the finger."

I cringed as he said those words. Growing up I had always lived by the code of the street, which is no snitching no matter what. During my teenage years I was in and out of juvenile detention centers and involved in street gangs. I joined the army with hopes of turning my life around. The only problem was that I never changed my old street mind-set. The desire to change was there, but I did not want to completely let go of the only life I had known. As a result I was constantly getting into trouble and I was involved in many fights off base. I never carried any weapons, but my behavior and the *decisions* I made were the leading cause of my current situation. Now I was at a crossroads, and I had to make another *decision*.

The detective saw me thinking about my answer. "Mr. Harvey, I know what you're thinking," he said. "We have spoken with several people about you, and we know that you and Sean were the leaders of a really tough group of soldiers. I want to tell you face-to-face that your old life is over. You need to make some drastic changes in your life right now because you have been given a second chance. No matter how you acted off base, you were still not supposed to be savagely attacked the way you were. You had no weapon and were defenseless against this man. We are going to charge him with attempted murder, so we hope to put him away for a long time. We just need your help, so you need to make a *decision* on which way you want to start this second chance at life."

I had to *decide* right then and there which way I was going to go. Was I going to stay true to the street mentality that had almost taken my life? Or was I going to choose to do the right thing and let the justice system handle this?

"I will let you know which one he is," I replied to the detective.

"Good *decision*," Detective Thomas remarked.

Detective Thomas handed me a stack of photos. I began thumbing through them one by one. Inside, I knew I was doing the right thing finally, but there was still that little voice telling me not to. On about the sixth picture, I stopped and froze like a deer trapped in headlights. The hair on my arms and neck stood up, and I could feel my heart beating very fast. I was looking face-to-face with the man who stabbed me. There was no doubt in my mind that this was him. The image of the incident was frozen in my mind. My blood began to boil like hot lava. The anger and the rage were beginning to be overwhelming. This was the moment of truth; what would I *decide* to do?

"Detective Thomas, this is the man who stabbed me," I said quietly.

Detective Thomas replied, "Are you 100 percent sure?"

I just shook my head yes. I had done it. I officially broke a code that I had lived by most of my life. However, deep down inside, I felt a sense of relief.

He handed me a pen and told me to circle his picture and sign the bottom of the paper. I did as he ordered.

"You made the right *decision*, Mr. Harvey," he said. "We are going to prosecute him to the fullest extent of the law!" He picked up his briefcase, shook my hand, and walked out the door.

I was left alone again in the room with my thoughts. The incident was now vividly playing in my mind. I wanted it to stop, but this just opened up the mental wound that I had been trying to cover up. Again, I just wanted to go to sleep so I didn't have to think about it.

HOPE

There were dead bodies everywhere. The smell from the rotting corpses overpowered my senses. I was trapped in a pit in the dark. I was slowly climbing my way forward toward the unknown. The light from the moon illuminated the partially decayed faces underneath me. There seemed to be no way out of this horrific situation.

"Help me!" I screamed in the dark. "Somebody, help me!" But there was no one there. I was alone; my heart was beating out of my chest. I began to struggle as hard as I could to get out of this hell!

Just then, I shook awake, my body was covered in sweat. It was dark in the hospital room; the only light came from the space under the door. "It was only a dream," I said as I exhaled. I took a deep breathe through my nose, and was horrified by what I smelled. The overwhelming aroma of death was in the air. The odor I smelled in my dream came from me. I began to panic. Why did I smell like a dead body? I reached around in the dark to find the call button to summon the nurse. I finally found it tucked under my covers, and I pushed the button.

The alarm began to beep loudly. I sat there in the dark for a minute, trying not to breathe through my nose.

Suddenly, the darkness was interrupted when the door swung open, and in walked my nurse. She turned on the light and was taken aback by the intense odor in the air. She came over to me and in a thick German accent told me that this was not good. She put her hand behind me and proceeded to sit me up to inspect my wounds. When I was in the upright position, my nurse looked at my back and gasped at the sight of my wounds. They were infected and swollen to the size of golf balls. She gently set me back and walked out of the room to get some assistance. Again, I was alone in the room. My wife was at home with her family getting some rest, and my mother was in her hotel room taking a shower and changing her clothes. I could not get over this horrible smell and the fear of what was going on with me. Not being able to communicate with my nurses and doctors made the whole experience that much worse because I never knew what they were doing. Finally, she came back into the room with another nurse to assist her. They wheeled in a small cart that carried medical supplies. At this point, I was still unsure of what was going on. Luckily, the second nurse that came in spoke a little more English than the first. She told me that the smell was coming from an infection in my wounds.

There was immense pressure in my upper back. The nurses peeled the dressings off slowly, which felt like they were ripping my skin off. They stood behind me and conversed in German. I wished so badly that I could understand what they were saying about my situation. Then I felt their hands around one of the wounds in my upper back. They began to apply pressure from both sides; all of a sudden, I felt a stream of liquid pour down my back. All I knew was that I was glad I could not see what my wounds looked like because the smell had just gotten even worse. They continued to apply intense pressure to each individual wound, and I could feel massive fluid being released all over my back. The smell grew worse and worse the longer they worked.

About ten minutes into the cleaning, my mother walked in, and she too was taken aback by the smell. She looked very concerned the further she walked into the room. I was so glad that there was finally someone I could communicate with.

"What in the world is going on?" she questioned.

"I think everything got infected," I replied.

She walked over to the nurses and said, "Oh my God! Yes, they are infected, Arnold." My mother's maternal instinct coupled with her years of nursing experience made her very concerned. This infection was worse than I originally thought, and now I was in another life-threatening situation. This had to be attended to correctly, or I could die. It was amazing to see my mother take control the way she did. She moved with purpose and conviction. She demonstrated to me what leadership looked like. I was really proud to be her son and felt blessed that she was my mother.

The cleaning process dragged on for what seemed like an eternity. I was in terrible pain throughout the entire ordeal.

They worked on me for at least an hour, but finally they were done, and I could go back to sleep.

The next morning, the doctors came in and did an examination of the wounds. My wife was still not back yet, so I sat there, listening to them discuss my situation in German. I was so ready to be transported to a military hospital where my doctors would speak English. They talked for a while and wrote some things down on their clipboards and left.

Right after they exited, the physical therapist walked in. I thought to myself that there was no way I was going to do any physical therapy after what happened last night. The one good thing was that I knew she spoke a fair amount of English, so we could communicate with each other. She came over to my bedside and told me that she wanted me to work on, trying to move my legs again. I was really not in the mood to go through this again. Every time we did these exercises, I ended up getting seriously frustrated. She insisted that we do at least fifteen minutes of focusing on wiggling my toes.

"Now I want you to concentrate on moving your big toe," she said.

I sat there straining for a few minutes and stopped. "It's not going to move," I told her. "I don't feel like trying right now!"

"Mr. Harvey, just try one more time," she insisted.

At this point, I was so angry that I thought about cussing her out. I gathered all my anger into one last push. I gave it everything I had and pushed as hard as I could. All of a sudden, my leg flinched!

"Did I do that?" I said excitedly.

"I'm not sure, try what you just did one more time," she replied.

I gathered up all of my strength once more, and pushed as hard as I could. It flinched again! This was the first time since the injury that I had hope of walking again. Before this, I had pretty much come to grips with the fact that I was going to be confined to a wheelchair. But now was a different story; there was finally hope for walking. Right then and there, I made a *decision* that I was going to walk again no matter what it took. In my mind, I could now see a better future than I had previously envisioned for myself. The *decision* I made while lying there came from deep within my soul. I knew in my heart that it was a long shot, but I was willing to swing the bat. The road ahead was not going to be easy, and it was going to take a new level of determination that I had never known before. I thought to myself, *What are my other options at that point?* I could continue to feel sorry for myself and be confined to a chair for the rest of my life. Or I could take on the mind-set of a warrior and not take this lying down. I had lost the battle, but I *decided* that I was going to win the war.

Shortly thereafter, my wife and mother came into the room, and I let them know the good news. I told them about my new goal to walk, and they both were very excited about the possibility. They both encouraged me by telling me that they knew I could do it. We talked about how great it would be to hold my daughter's hand and walk her to the bus stop. Never once was there any talk about me not being able to do it. I believed that I could do it. The vision of success was vivid in my mind. We discussed the time frame that I wanted to complete my goal in. We wanted to set some realistic goals for my future. I *decided* that I would walk out of the hospital with no support in one year. Once we finished talking about that, I was filled in on the fact that we were going to get ready to move to me to a military hospital in Landstuhl. My German doctors were amazing people who saved my life. They did an absolutely incredible job of stabilizing me, the only issue I had was our lack of ability to communicate with one another. The move was very exciting news to me it meant that I would be able to fully understand everything that was going on with my care.

The move went off without a hitch. My wife and mother came with me. I was so happy to finally be in an American hospital. I was able to talk with the doctors for the first time. The doctors ran so many tests on me that I felt like a guinea pig. I had about a half a dozen blood tests, several X-rays, a CAT scan, and an MRI. I was told that my injury was very unique and rare because usually, the entire spinal cord is either crushed or severed. My injury was a one-in-a-million-type injury, and most of the doctors had never seen a partial sever before. They would come in with groups of doctors at different times to ask me all sorts of questions about what I could and couldn't feel.

I was told that the infection I went through was definitely life-threatening. There is a chance that it could have damaged the spinal cord further. They told me we wouldn't be able to tell until later on in my recovery. They took great care of me there. All the doctors and nurses were amazing. The nurses spent a considerable amount of time working on the wounds by dressing and cleaning them out very often. Over time, I really grew to hate medical tape. It hurt so bad taking it off that it became my archenemy.

I stayed in Landstuhl for a week or so. Eventually, it was time to go, and I got ready for my flight to Walter Reed hospital in Washington DC. The move to DC was amazing news because I am originally from the Washington DC metropolitan area. I grew up about twenty-five miles from the hospital, so I would be able to see my family often. The move also came with sadness, however. The problem was that my wife wasn't going to be able to fly with us because she was pregnant. The doctors informed me that she wouldn't be able to make the trip until the baby was at least three months old. We were both upset with the fact that I wasn't going to be able to see the birth. We struggled with the fact that she was going to have to go through it by herself. We talked for a while and came to terms with the situation. What could we do about it? We had to do what we had to do. We made plans for her to come to the United States. I promised my wife that I would have an apartment set up and ready for her and the baby.

The flight to Walter Reed was different, to say the least. Two soldiers came to get me and wheeled me out on to the tarmac of the airport. There was a huge cargo plane parked with its enormous back door wide open. The soldiers wheeled me on board where I saw cots lining the walls of the plane.

As we rolled down the middle of the plane, I saw many other injured soldiers lying down with IV bags hanging above them. I asked my escort where all these soldiers were coming from. The soldier wheeling me told me that these were soldiers that were injured fighting in Afghanistan. The soldier stopped the wheelchair next to an empty cot to my right that was about three feet off the ground. They picked me up and put me on the cot. One soldier grabbed under my shoulders, the other picked up my legs. Once on the cot, I looked around, and I was amazed at how many people were lining the walls of the plane. To my left on the opposite wall, there was a young man who was severely injured. There was a bag of blood next to the IV bag hanging from above his cot. His face was severely burned, and it looked like he was missing a leg. I started to understand and see that I was blessed to be alive.

DETERMINATION

A thick cloud of despair loomed over Walter Reed Hospital when I arrived. Everywhere I looked there were young men and women in pain. As we wheeled down the hallway, we passed soldier after soldier missing arms, legs, and many were severely burned. The sadness around this place was infectious. There were many family members in the waiting area crying and hugging one another. I could sense death around every corner. The war in Afghanistan was raging. Walter Reed was the main stop for most of the soldiers returning from battle. It was so sad to see so many young people were severely injured.

I finally reached my room in the hospital. I was so relieved to see my bed. I had been traveling for over thirteen hours, and I was exhausted. Next to me there was a young man lying asleep. Once I got settled in and finally lay down to rest, the young man awoke.

"Hey, buddy, my name is Chris," he said. "I guess we are roommates now," he said with a smile.

"Guess so, my name is Arnold. It's nice to meet you Chris," I replied.

"What happened to you?" Chris asked. "What part of Afghanistan were you in?"

"I wasn't in the war, I was injured in Germany," I answered.

Chris looked puzzled. "Were you hurt in a training mission or something?"

I was a little put off by the amount of questions he was asking, but I figured he was just being a nice guy who wanted to strike up conversation. "I was stabbed by another soldier off post," I told him. "One of the stab wounds hit my spinal cord, so I'm paralyzed from the chest down."

"What? That's crazy!" Chris exclaimed. "That really sucks, dude, I'm sorry to hear that," he continued.

"It's all good man," I responded. "What happened to you?"

"I was hit by a roadside bomb and lost both of my legs." As he spoke, he removed the blanket from his lower half, revealing his amputated legs. One was missing from just above the knee and the other was closer to the hip. "I'm the lucky one though," he continued. "I lost my good friend who was driving the Humvee. The truck rolled when we were hit, and he broke his neck and died."

I could see the pain set in as he spoke about his friend. His eyes began to water, and his voice began to crack. You could tell that he was reliving the horrible scene.

"I am so sorry to hear that, man," I replied. "Well, we are both here for a reason. I'm not sure why, but we are here."

"You're right, Arnold," responded Chris. "Everyone said there was no way anyone should have survived that explosion. So someone is watching over us."

After that, Chris and I lay down on our beds silently. My mind started to replay all the images of injured soldiers I had encountered thus far in my journey. I thought back to the many cots lining the walls of the cargo plane I was on. As well as the dozens of soldiers I passed in the hallway on the way to my room. Now I just heard another story of horrific tragedy from my roommate. My *reality* was really starting to set in at this point. Up until now, I was in complete survival mode. I was fighting for my life in the other two hospitals, but now, I was more or less stable. I now understood completely that this was my life, and that this was going to be a serious battle. At that point, I unknowingly made a *decision*. I *decided* right then and there that I was going to let the sadness and depression to start to creep in. I just as well could have *decided* to stay strong and remain positive and optimistic. As I lay awake on my bed, I was overtaken by depression once again and just wanted to go to sleep.

The next morning, I awoke to see five doctors in lab coats, carrying clipboards in my room.

"Mr. Harvey," one of the doctors said. "Good morning, sir, I hope you were able to get some rest after your long flight."

I sat up and rubbed my eyes. "Yes, sir, thank you. I did."

"We have some bad news for you, Mr. Harvey," one of the others said. "Your records were lost during your transport, and we are going to have to run all of the tests over again to create a new file on you. We are terribly sorry that this happened, but there is nothing we can do."

This really upset me because I had been prodded and poked so many times in the last couple of weeks. This was really going to suck! The sadness that started to settle in the night before was just magnified with this news. Nothing could go smoothly for me. Everything had to be so difficult throughout this whole ordeal. I could not get a break. At this point, I was truly depressed.

"Do whatever you have to do, sir," I said despondently.

"Also, with the rarity of your condition, we want our students to accompany us during your tests, for educational purposes," said one doctor. "Would that be alright with you, Mr. Harvey?"

You have to be kidding me! I thought to myself. *Now you want me to be your little test monkey for your students too?* I wanted to go off on this guy so bad, but all the doctors were officers, and I was just a private. Even though I didn't want the students in the room, there was nothing I could do about it. I just shrugged my shoulders to signify my submission. I really just didn't care anymore.

I spent the entire day being poked with needle after needle. In and out of MRI and CAT scan machines once again. They asked me a million questions and took pages of notes. I felt like I was some kind of science experiment. It was way more intense and thorough than the full exam I went through in Landstuhl, Germany. My reality was getting worse by the minute. I just wanted to go back to my room and go to sleep. My back hurt, my arm hurt, my mind hurt, and my heart hurt. Why wouldn't everyone just leave me alone? Why do

I have to suffer again for their mistakes? I was beginning to dwell in the pain of the situation. Everything was out of my control. The frustration with life was really beginning to set in. I became very angry at this point.

I made it through the tests that day and got back to my room in the early evening. I was mentally and physically exhausted when my nurse entered the room. She came in the door with a bright smile on her face, and that really irritated me. *Why is she so happy?* I thought. *Can't she see all of this pain around her?*

"Mr. Harvey, I have good news," she said gleefully. "I just received word that your family is coming for a visit in about twenty minutes!"

Normally, that would have excited me. But at this point, I was in full-blown depression. I really didn't want to see them. I knew I was going to have to talk for the next couple of hours. I didn't respond to her.

"Are you all right, sir?" she inquired. "I thought you would be happy to see them. I understand you haven't seen them since your injury."

I made myself respond. "I am just tired."

"I can call them back and tell them that you're not up to having company," she continued.

I seriously thought about having them turn around and go back. Then I started to think about the fact that it was cold and dark outside, and they were already on the road, so I could not bring myself to do it.

"No, that's fine. They can come," I said begrudgingly.

"Okay, well, I will let you know as soon as they arrive," the nurse said as she walked out of the door.

I honestly did not want to see anyone. I had made the *decision* already that I was going to feel sorry for myself. I didn't want anyone to try and cheer me up. That last thing I wanted to do was sit down with my family and hear them talk about how I should be thanking God for being alive. I really wasn't too happy with God at this point.

Twenty minutes later, I got a knock at my door. I immediately got a nervous feeling in the pit of my stomach. I knew that my family had made it. I was going to see my brother and sisters for the first time since the incident.

"Come in," I said nervously.

"Mr. Harvey, your family is here to see you," said my nurse.

"Okay, they can come in," I replied.

In walked my entire family with gifts and smiles. In walked my brother Arthur along with my two sisters Angela and Rebecca. My mother and father followed. It actually felt good to see them all come in. I had imagined it to be a bad experience in my mind. Surprisingly, my spirits were immediately lifted a little when I saw all their faces. They all came in and grabbed seats. We talked for about an hour and a half about everything. We laughed and joked the whole time. I ended up feeling so much better about my life by the time everyone was leaving. I was really shocked that my mood changed so much when I was around the people that I love. I wasn't 100 percent happier, but I was at least moving in the right direction. I saw how important my family was to me and at that point I made another decision. I once again *decided* that I was going to pick myself up out of the dumps and move forward in my recovery.

The next day after my initial round of tests, I got a chance to lie back down in my bed for a much needed afternoon rest. I was in pretty good spirits, thanks to the visit from my family the night before. I needed to make the transfer from my wheelchair to my bed (which I had just learned to do the day before), and as I moved, I smelled the foul odor of a bowel movement. Up until this point, I had to wear Depends for when I would go to the bathroom. I also had a catheter inserted into my pubic area that went directly into my bladder for when I had to urinate. I was unable to tell when I had to go to the bathroom, which was terrible. The only way I would know would be by the smell afterwards. In Germany, my mother took over the cleaning duties, which was completely weird at first. As time went by, I eventually became okay with it. Usually when I used the bathroom, I would hit the call button, and a nurse would come in and take care of the mess. I was really getting tired of being changed like a little baby though. At the same time, I was starting to get physically stronger and knew one day I would be doing it on my own.

I sat up on the edge of the bed and hit the call button even though I really didn't want to. I laid flat on my back and got ready for the nurse to come in and do their thing. About two minutes went by when all of a sudden, the most beautiful nurse I had ever seen walked in. She could have been no older than thirty years old, and she was absolutely gorgeous by anyone's standards. I was devastated that this woman was about to change my dirty diaper like I was a little baby.

"Can I help you, Mr. Harvey?" said the beautiful nurse.

Oh my goodness, she sounds like an angel, I thought to myself. I froze for a moment, debating whether or not I should just stay like this until the shift changed or not. I looked up at the clock on the wall, and it was only eleven o clock. They still had another five hours at least before they changed shifts again.

"Umm, I…umm…," I stammered. *What should I say?* I thought.

By this time, she was close enough to smell what the problem was.

"Do you need to be changed, Mr. Harvey?" she inquired.

I just wanted to crawl under a rock and die at this point. Now she knew. There was nothing I could say. I closed my eyes in shame. She could tell that I was more than embarrassed at this point.

"Mr. Harvey, don't be embarrassed," she said lovingly. "This is part of my job, and I love being a nurse. I know this must be extremely hard for you, but don't worry, I will be done quickly."

Her words brought me no solace. I was once again on this emotional roller coaster that I could not manage to get off. I just kept my eyes closed the entire time. I could not bear to see this beautiful woman changing my diaper. She pulled my pants down and rolled me to my side to clean me up. As I lay there with my eyes closed and my back to her, I began to cry. The tears and the sadness turned into anger and *determination* in an instant. I was again at a crossroads in my life. All of me wanted to just give up. This was all too hard to deal with. Every time I would feel up for a little while, I would be knocked down ten steps farther. This time, I just had enough! *I will never have someone change my diaper again*! I thought to myself as I lay there crying. In that moment, I *decided* to put on my gloves again and step back in the ring with life. It would have been so much easier to quit in that moment and throw in the towel. I mean, I had already *decided* once before to fight, and I had given up. Why even try again, why get back up after being knocked down? I was so angry with life and God at this point that I wanted to show them that I could get back up and fight. Anger motivated me to make a *decision* to move forward and take control of my situation in whatever way I could. The nurse finished, and I rolled over and had a long deep cry. I needed to release all of the emotions that I had held in since the stabbing happened. I felt so relieved after the tears stopped. It felt like the knots in my soul were untied a little bit.

Two days passed before my next bowel movement. I was anxiously waiting for it to happen. I wanted to show the world that I was going to move forward with life. The moment of truth was here; game on! My stab wounds were still healing, and they were very sore at this point, and I was still very unsteady sitting up on my own. None of that mattered to me. I was going to do this. It was me against the world at this point. I was going in the bathroom, and I wasn't coming out until I had the victory. Now the thing was that I had no plan.

I didn't know how this was going to go down. I grabbed two packs of the wipes the nurses always used on me and took off my shirt and rolled myself in the bathroom.

Once in there, I had to try to figure out a way to get my pants off on my own. With me not being able to move my legs made it a serious challenge, but somehow I did it. I want to spare you from all of the nasty details. I'll just say I got everything off. My back was hurting so bad at this point, and I was starting to sweat profusely. I was off balance, so I almost flipped my wheelchair several times throughout this process. Everything was off, but now came the hard part because there was a mess everywhere. It was all over my chair, all over me, and all over the walls. It seemed like I might have to give up because I was beginning to be in excruciating pain. Just then, I heard a knock at the door.

"Mr. Harvey, is everything okay in there?" said the voice.

Decision time! I could have given up right then and got some help. I mean I had come a long way, hadn't I? I was hurting really bad, and this was going to take a long time for me to clean up all by myself. This was a critical *decision* for me to *m*ake. If I quit, I was going to tell myself that it was okay to give up when the pain set in. If I kept going, I was going to tell myself that I can push through the pain and do whatever I put my mind to.

"I'm fine!" I yelled. "I'll be out in a little while."

"Okay, let us know if you need help, sir," said the voice on the other side of the door.

I made the *decision* to fight through the pain. I felt a sense of power within me.

"I am going to beat this, and I don't care how bad it hurts or how long it takes," I whispered to myself. "I am coming out of this bathroom clean and changed, no matter what!"

I spent another hour in the bathroom sweating, hurting, and stinking. I must have flushed the toilet a hundred times. I had no concern for water conservation at this point. Finally, somehow I was done. I had defeated my Goliath. I felt like a victor. I went into battle and won. I reached for the door handle and opened the door. When the door opened, there were several nurses and a doctor standing there. As I rolled out, they began clapping for me. It was the most amazing feeling I had felt in a long time. *Determination* and persistence paid off for me. All of the pain was worth the amazing feeling I had at that moment. I was ready to move forward, and I was determined to walk again. I learned right there that it doesn't matter how many times you get knocked down; it matters how many times you get up.

RECOVERY

M y time at Walter Reed had finally come to an end. It was now time to move forward with my *recovery*. I was now being transferred to the McGuire's Veterans Hospital in Richmond, Virginia. This is one of the premier spinal cord injury facilities on the East Coast. Veterans and soldiers from all over the country are assigned there after they have been injured. They also have long-term patients who have been injured for several years.

The day the van pulled up was absolutely gorgeous. The sun was shining bright, and you could tell that the cold winter was nearing its end. I arrived at McGuire's at the very end of February, which was almost a full month since my injury took place. I could feel that I was getting stronger as each day passed. I could now sit up by myself and transfer from my chair to the bed alone. The small victory I had in the bathroom of Walter Reed had me feeling like I could conquer the world. I knew that beyond a shadow of a doubt that I was going to be walking out of there when I left.

I got off the ramp on the van and started rolling my way up to the door of the hospital. Outside in the front patio area sat about a half a dozen older veterans in wheelchairs, talking and smoking cigarettes. Some of them were in the larger motorized chairs while others were in the smaller pushchairs like mine. As I rolled up, I could sense the feeling around there was much lighter than the heavy dark feeling at Walter Reed.

"Hey, young blood!" shouted one of the older vets. "Looking good there, you coming to live with us for a little while?"

"Yes, sir," I replied. "Today is my first day, seems like a nice place."

"Oh yeah, the doctors and nurses here are great!" said another veteran. "You'll like it here I'm sure."

I continued rolling by them and entered the big electronic sliding doors that led into a side hallway of the hospital. I was feeling really good about this place. Everybody seemed to be in pretty good spirits. Nurses and doctors were zooming by in the hallway. They all gave me a little smile as they passed, and I returned one to them. I continued out into the main hallway and was met by a young lady.

"I'm assuming that you are, Arnold Harvey," she said with a smile.

"That would be me, ma'am," I replied.

"Please don't call me ma'am. You're making me feel old," she said as she laughed. "Call me Nicole. I will take you to your ward where you will meet your doctors and nurses. Do you need me to push you down the hall?"

"No, I'm good," I said with my head held high and my chest out.

When we got to the ward, there was a small group of doctors and nurses congregating around a large semicircle desk in between two hallways. I was really excited to meet everybody and to get this show on the road. As we approached, one of the doctors facing us acknowledged Nicole and me, which made them all turn around to face us. Every one of them had a smile on their face, and they were very warm and inviting.

Each one approached me and introduced themselves with their name and their occupation. I had a very large team of different professionals that were going to be working with me. I had a neurosurgeon, a physical therapist, an occupational therapist, a primary care doctor, a psychiatrist, and a social worker on my team. I was very surprised to see how many different doctors and nurses I would be working with. I felt really special for there to be such a fuss over me. Once introductions were over, we went over what the goals of the team were and what kind of treatment I would get from each individual.

After we were done and the group broke to go handle their normal duties, I knew that I was going to like it here, and this was the best shot I had to get up out of this chair. Nicole proceeded to show me where my room was. We entered into a large room with four beds inside. The beds were set up two on each half of the room. Each bed had a large padded rocking chair sitting next to it as well as a wall locker for personal items. Each bed was nicely made with a small TV set suspended from the ceiling by a retractable arm. The sun was shining brightly through the large wall of windows to the far side of the room.

"This is your bed, Arnold," Nicole said. "This is the locker that you can put your stuff in, just make sure you use the lock provided and keep the key that's on the string around your neck."

I couldn't help but to smile. It reminded me of being in basic training all over again minus the yelling from the drill sergeants. They were the exact same lockers I used in Fort Knox three years earlier. A flood of images went through my mind of the time I spent in the freezing Kentucky winter, learning how to be a soldier. I thought back to a time when I was in the best physical shape of my life. I remembered having a sixty-pound rucksack on my back and marching for what seemed like an eternity in the snow. We would do hundreds of sit-ups and push-ups and run for miles and miles. I snapped back to the reality of me being in the hospital and sitting in a wheelchair. This time was different though; this time, I *decided* to use the thoughts as motivation instead of getting depressed. I knew that I may never get back to the old me, but I was going to get as close to it as I possibly could.

After I got settled in, Nicole left, and evening began creeping in. The sun that was shining bright earlier began going down. I lay down on my bed and turned the TV on. Just as I got, comfortable in came my roommates. They were finished with their appointments for the day and were getting ready for dinner. All three of them were older gray-haired gentlemen in motorized wheelchairs. Two of them I found out were paraplegics, and the third was a quadriplegic. It was amazing to be around other people who had the same type of injury as I had. We all four talked for quite some time, and they shared with me their experiences of being paralyzed. I was determined to not be in my chair for long after I heard them talk about it. I came away from our conversation with a ton of respect for anyone who lives their life in a wheelchair.

Soon after I got acclimated to life at the VA Hospital, I began physical therapy. I was so excited to finally start working out. It really felt like I was moving forward with life. I met my therapists, and they were all great people. They were a smiling bunch and were always happy and enthusiastic about life in general. At the beginning of therapy, we focused mainly on upper-body strengthening. For the legs and lower body, we did mostly stretching exercises along with working on dexterity. I was getting stronger and stronger with each workout session. I began to have more movement in my right leg, but my left leg lagged behind. Feeling started to come back very slowly. The feeling that did return was very sporadic and painful in certain areas. My therapists and I talked many times about the possibility of walking again. Everyone was very optimistic about my chances; they just didn't know how well I would be able to walk.

About a week into therapy I was lying in bed after a long day of working out when my bedside telephone rang. I answered it and heard my wife on the other end. We spoke nearly every day, so I assumed it was just going to be one of our regular conversations. However, this was not a routine call; she was in full-blown labor.

"Arnold, the baby is coming today," she said while breathing very hard.

"Oh my God," I said surprised. "Are you okay?"

"Yes I'm fine," she said. "I just wish you were here with me. My mother is getting the car ready now to take me to the hospital."

"I wish I was there too, baby," I said solemnly. "I love you, and I know everything is going to go smoothly and you and the baby will be fine."

"I love you too," she replied. "My mom is ready, sweetie, I will call you when the baby comes."

"All right, baby, be strong," I said.

I sat there in my bed and thought about the fact that I was going to be a father. I was actually going to have a baby. It was finally about to happen. I easily could have gotten upset with the fact that I wasn't going to be there, but I *decided* that I was going to be grateful that I was alive to see my child.

I stayed up for as long as I could that night to get the call saying that the baby was born. Around midnight, I fell asleep and had a dream about what my new baby was going to look like. I was woken up around four in the morning by one of the nurses on night shift.

"Arnold, wake up. Your wife had the baby," she said while shaking me awake.

I sat up quickly and cleared my throat. "Really, the baby is here?" I questioned.

"Yes, sir, we just received a call letting us know that your wife and the baby are both doing well," she said softly. "Your baby weighed in at a healthy seven pounds, eleven ounces. They are both resting peacefully, and your wife will give you a call tomorrow."

"Thank you," I said with a smile. *I'm a daddy*, I thought. *I have a healthy baby girl!* This was one of the proudest moments of my life. I was so grateful to have survived my ordeal and to have the chance to raise my little girl. I envisioned a future with me walking her to the bus stop and playing with her outside. This just lit a new fire in me that was a billion times bigger than the fire I had previously. Now there was absolutely no doubt that I would walk out of there.

The next day I got a call around midmorning from my wife. She was in great spirits, and we talked for a long time. She told me about the whole experience. She had actually been through a great deal during the childbirth. There was a mix-up at the hospital, and she ended up having the baby with no anesthesia. She described to me the pain she had to go through. I felt so bad for her but told me how it was all so worth it. Our little girl came out healthy and beautiful. Tracy's mother took tons of pictures and was working on getting them e-mailed to me. I was so proud and excited throughout our whole conversation. I hung up the phone with tears of pride and joy in my eyes. I went to the nurses' station with great anticipation of finally seeing my daughter for the first time.

After about forty-five minutes, the first pictures came in. She looked like a wrinkly little Eskimo baby. I had the nurses print out a couple of the best pictures that we received, and I showed them to whoever would look. The fact that I was in a wheelchair at that point did not even matter. I knew that it was temporary, and I would walk with my little girl.

The weeks started to pass by faster and faster. I was now set into a regular routine, and I was getting stronger each day. The motivation for walking drove me to push myself to the limit. Although I have to admit that there were some days that I had to be coaxed out of bed by my doctors. The strength and mobility of my right leg was now leaps and bounds ahead of my left. I hadn't regained any muscular activity in my calf, hamstring, as well as the muscle that lifts my foot on my left side. None of that mattered to me though because I felt blessed with the amount of movement I had. I looked around and saw that none of the other vets on my ward had half as much mobility as me, which made me very grateful. Most of their injuries were what is called complete; their spinal cords had either been crushed or severed completely.

The moment of truth had finally come for me. I was strong enough to try and stand for the first time. The therapist had my chair pulled up to two parallel bars. He put a support belt around my waist in case I fell. I got my courage up and grabbed the bars. Slowly, I pulled myself up out of the chair. It was the most amazing experience for me. I was doing what all of the doctors told me I would never do. I told my therapist to let me go, I wanted to stand on my own. Inch by inch, my back straightened out, and finally I stood up straight.

Every day from there on out I would be on those parallel bars. I worked my hardest each chance I got to move one step closer to my goal of walking. When I would be back in my room, I would reach for things from my chair and forget that I could stand and get them. Eventually, I became accustomed to it and started standing every opportunity I got. My nurses were not too happy about that. They would walk in and catch me standing up brushing my teeth and rush over to me in a panic. They would tell me that I needed to sit down because I could fall and hurt myself. I would listen as long as they were around, but as soon as they left, I was right back up. I could feel that I was getting closer to my goal every day.

At the same time, I was starting to get some feeling back in my bladder, and they were finally able to remove the catheter. They taught me how to catheterize myself, but that was not how I wanted to live my life either. I wanted to go to the bathroom on my own, and after a couple weeks, I was able to accomplish that goal as well.

As time passed, I started to be able to walk with a walker as long as a therapist was holding on to me. Eventually, the therapist would let go, and I would take several steps on my own. That then led to me walking with a three-point cane. I would walk up and down the long hallways repeatedly. Throughout this whole process, I always had excruciating pain in my left foot and lower back. I have severe neurological pain in my foot that felt like I was walking on broken glass, but I pushed through it.

There was a handicapped driving course at the hospital, and I took full advantage of it. My right leg was now at about 70 percent, so I felt comfortable driving regularly instead of using the hand controls that most people with paralysis use. It took about two weeks of practicing, but I was cleared to drive. This was another big moment for me because I felt like I was becoming a little more "normal."

By the time I was ready to go, I was walking almost everywhere I went. The other veterans told me I shouldn't do that because I might not get as much money for my disability. I told them they could keep the check. I wanted to walk. The time came for me to be released. Before I was released, I had to go through a three-day test. There was a space in the hospital that was set up like an apartment, and I had to live there on my own for three days. I passed the test with flying colors. After the test was over, I packed my stuff and got ready to be released. I walked down my ward and said my good-byes to all the staff. I was really going to miss them. They were all great to me, and I am thankful that God put me in such a caring environment. I made my last walk through the double doors without my cane. I was really wobbly with no support, but I wanted to do what I said I was going to do. I walked out of the hospital four months after I was stabbed twelve times and paralyzed from the chest down. Now was time for the real world. I thought I was ready.

REALITY

Walking out of the hospital was my Olympic gold medal. My mind, body, and soul were consumed with that goal. I thought about nothing other than accomplishing what I had set out to do. The thought of life after I succeeded really never crossed my mind. But here it was, whether I was ready or not. Being in the hospital, you are in a very safe environment that is created to help you move about easily. The real world is dangerous and scary, and nothing is created for the ease and comfort of the handicapped. I could stand and walk a little, but I wasn't that strong or steady yet. I needed my walker to move around, and I could only walk short distances before I was in excruciating pain.

I got to my parents' house about two hours after I left the hospital. It was great to see the house I had grown up in since seventh grade. I got out of the car and my mother handed me my walker. I made my way up the step to get to the door with no problem. Once inside, I looked around, and the sweet smell of home was in the air. I walked through the house slowly and was amazed to see how much it had changed in the last year since I had been home. I sat down and talked with the family for a while and had to figure out where I would sleep. I wanted the room upstairs. The only other option was putting a bed downstairs in the family area. There was no way that was going to happen. I had gotten pretty good going upstairs while I was in the hospital. My right leg was getting really strong and could bear my weight going up. My family wasn't too excited about me going up- and downstairs, but of course I wanted to do it and won the debate. I managed quite well getting up and down to my room. I would come down once in the morning and go up to get into bed.

I had no time to get comfortable though. My wife and daughter were getting ready to come in two weeks. The doctors required them to wait until the baby could fly, and now was the time. The three months had flown by in the blink of an eye. I could not believe that I was finally going to see them. I wanted to live somewhere close to the hospital that had public transportation. I found a place that was perfect. It was really close to Walter Reed, and the apartment was in a really nice area that was growing. The problem was it was about twenty-five minutes away from my parents' house. My mother and father were very supportive of the move and spent a lot of time driving miles to get everything set up. It was such a great place right in the middle of downtown. It had a beautiful lobby and was very accessible by wheelchair. I was close to all of the stores and shops, which made it great because I wouldn't have to drive everywhere. I could just wheel myself right out of the lobby and be able to shop around. The only issue was the price was completely out of my range. I made the mistake of overlooking that issue and moved in anyway.

The apartment was finally ready just in time for my family to fly in. We met my wife and three-month-old daughter at the airport. I was standing tall as they walked towards us. My wife was overjoyed to see me standing, and I was beyond excited to see my baby. We hugged and cried a little while I held my little girl for the first time. I was so relieved to have them here with me. I finally had my family.

For the first couple weeks, life was great. I was assigned to the medical hold unit at Walter Reed, so all I had to do was check in by phone every morning. That really gave me a lot of time to bond with my girl. She was so beautiful. She was the joy of my life and perfect in every way. The hardest adjustment was with my wife because life was really different now for her. I wasn't able to really do that much around the house because of the chronic pain I was experiencing in my foot and back. My nerve endings were firing at a million miles a second, and the pain was unbearable. I spent a lot of time lying down with my foot elevated. Also, at night, I would have constant accidents, which were so embarrassing. We were really working on adjusting to our new *reality*.

However, as time went on, we started to get into a lot of arguments. Tempers were starting to flare. I had a really short fuse that I would always blame on the pain both physically and mentally. Along with the physical pain, I began having some very terrible nightmares several times a week, and

I did not like being around a lot of people. I really started to shut myself off in the apartment for the majority of each day. What I didn't realize back then was that it wasn't the pain that caused me to be angry and short-tempered. It had nothing to do with the circumstances I was faced with at all. Everything was a direct result of the *decision* I made at the time to deal with the situation. I could have just as easily *decided* to react differently to the pain. There were many other avenues I could have chosen to take advantage of throughout my ordeal. Instead of snapping at my wife, I could have took the time and told her how I was feeling. I look back now and see how I had all the opportunity in the world to lie down and pray or meditate, which I was taught to do at the VA hospital. I could have talked to my doctors and told them about what was going on. Instead I *decided* to keep it all bottled up and took it out on my wife. I chose to turn my pain into anger, which started to destroy my marriage slowly. The stress of our limited finances began to weigh heavy on us as well. The apartment I *decided* to move into was completely out of our budget. After paying the rent and bills, we barely had any money left over for the month. This stemmed from another bad *decision* that I made. I knew when I saw this place that it was going to be too expensive for us, but I *decided* to go ahead with it anyway. I did not understand that every *decision* I made mattered.

Around two months into my new *reality*, I received a call from Germany. On the other end of the line there was a US Army captain who wanted to speak to me about something important.

"Is this Mr. Harvey?" he asked

"Yes, sir, it is," I replied.

"This is Captain James," he continued. "I will be representing you in the case against Private Johnson."

My heart started to race the moment he said my attacker's name. I had been trying my hardest to forget about the incident all together. Every time I thought about it, I would get very anxious, and my hands would get all clammy and start to sweat. I was still having nightmares quite often that were so terrifying I would wake up drenched with sweat. Needless to say, the less I thought about it, the better I felt.

"We are going to need you to fly to Germany, Mr. Harvey," continued the captain. "We are going to be taking Private Johnson to trial for attempted murder."

My palms began to sweat as my heart rate picked up even more. Images of Johnson's face flooded my mind. My scars started to ache as I replayed the attack in my mind.

"Are you there, Private Harvey?" the captain questioned.

I snapped back to reality. "Yes, sir, I am here. When do I have to be there?"

"We have a flight set up for you a week from today," he said. "We have your hotel reservations and everything already taken care of. We are going to try and make your trip as comfortable for you as we can. We understand that you have been through a lot in the last couple of months. We also know that this is not going to be easy for you to go through. There will be a therapist working with you throughout the trial, so if there are some things you need to talk about, you can always talk to her."

The day that I dreaded and hoped for at the same time was now right around the corner. "Yes, sir," I replied. "Just let me know what I need to do and where I need to go."

I was met at the German airport by two soldiers that were responsible for bringing me to my hotel room. It was a bittersweet moment returning to Germany. I absolutely love Germany. I had always planned on living there after I got out of the service. I loved the environment as well as the people. Seeing all of the German signs brought back great memories of traveling around Europe with my friends. In the back of my mind, I knew that this trip was not for pleasure. This was going to be one of the hardest things I had ever done.

The weather was absolutely gorgeous when I got there. It was early summer, so it was not too hot or too cold. We got to the hotel, and the soldiers carried my bags for me to the room. I was in my wheelchair, but I brought my walker with me to get around the room. After the two soldiers left, I figured I might as well enjoy the beautiful day, so I took a long stroll down the sidewalk in the city. There were Germans and Americans bustling all around me, and I felt that warm feeling of being home. For a couple of hours, I didn't even think about the real reason why I was there.

The next day, I was escorted to the base where I was to meet my new legal team. I was introduced to Captain James and his staff. At first glance, I was really disappointed when I saw Captain James. He looked very young and did not really resemble a powerful attorney with a lot of experience. His demeanor was somewhat timid. He did not display a lot of confidence at all. I learned that Captain James just graduated from school and that this was going to be his first major case. This was a real concern for me seeing as how Johnson was able to get an outside attorney. I was sure he would have a good one because he was facing life in prison.

For the first time, I was shown police photographs taken directly after the incident had taken place when I was still in a coma. They were horrible. I looked like I was dead. One of the pictures was a close-up of my face. I had no color at all and was lying on a metal bed. It looked like they were getting ready to embalm me. After we went through the pictures, we began going over the incident to see what I could remember. This was the hard part because not only did I have to describe the incident out loud, I also had to answer in-depth questions about it. Captain James wanted to know every little detail. He wanted to know who was standing where, how they were standing, which way they were facing, etc. He told me that it was very important to know all these things because the defense attorney was going to try and trip me up. We went over the entire scene at least five times to make sure I had it down pat.

After we went over the scene, Captain James explained to me that the defense attorney was most likely going to bring up my past and paint the picture of me as an aggressive violent person. He was going to claim that his client was trying to protect himself against my attacks. I made some really bad *decisions* while I was in the army. There were always a lot of fights between drunk soldiers off post. I just so happened to be involved in many of them. I hung out with some other soldiers that had the same street mentality that I had, but nobody ever used weapons. I fought so much at one club that the owner asked me if I wanted a job as a bouncer. I gladly took it. I was now getting paid to break up fights and get physical. The *decisions* I made were bad, but it didn't mean I deserved to be stabbed the way I was.

When I left the captain's office that day, I was more nervous and anxious than I had ever been. I was already upset about the fact that I was getting ready to face Johnson, and now I knew that they were going to try to make me look like some kind of monster. I wanted to go home so badly. I absolutely did not want to go through with this. My mind told me no, but my heart told me that this is what I had to do.

That night, I had one of the most terrifying nightmares I had ever had. It was one of those nightmares where I knew that I was asleep but my body was completely paralyzed and Johnson was in my room with a knife. It was so real to me. I was more scared than I had ever been. I couldn't wake up, and he was coming to stab me again. I struggled so hard to break the paralysis, but I was frozen. Johnson was now standing over me with a massive knife. He bent down and put the knife to my throat. He said, "If you tell on me, I will kill your daughter." I did everything I could to wake up but not a muscle would move. He then took the knife and slowly drove it into my stomach inch by agonizing inch. I could actually feel the blade entering me. Finally after what seemed like an eternity, I was able to break free from nightmare. I woke up in a pool of sweat. I looked around the room to make sure he wasn't there. I looked at the clock and saw I had an hour before I was to get up for court.

We arrived right on time for court the next morning. I was still despondent from the nightmare the night before. I met with Captain James, and he looked a little shaky and nervous. We briefly went over my testimony and made our way up to the courtroom. I was then told by the judge that I was not allowed to be present for the proceedings because the eyewitness reports might change my thoughts on what took place. I was then secluded to a small room where I sat alone quietly for about two hours, which seemed like two days. It was just me and a chair and a desk and some reading material. I read magazines the whole time to keep my mind off the situation. Captain James would come back and check on me from time to time and bring me some soda and chips. Then all of a sudden, a familiar face showed up. It was Sean. We hadn't seen each other since the stabbing. We talked for a long while and caught up with each other. Apparently, Sean got very lucky because the knife didn't hit anything vital. He had some scars, but that was about it. He told me how sorry he was that I was injured so badly. I told him that I was just grateful that I was alive. Then the bailiff called him in to testify.

Sean finished, and it was finally my turn to go into the courtroom. The bailiff came back and got me. He wheeled me up to the two solid oak doors. The anxiety reached its highest point as the doors opened. The courtroom was filled to capacity when I rolled my way in. Johnson's face was hidden from view initially. As I was rolled in farther, the obstruction was no longer blocking him, and there he was. He had his full military uniform on. His face was exactly as I remembered it in my nightmares. The room started to spin a little bit for me at this point. I felt like I was going to pass out. The bailiff continued to roll me up to the witness stand. He rolled me all the way up to it and turned my chair to face the audience. Johnson and I made eye contact for the first time since the night of the attack. I told myself before coming that I was not going to look away when I saw him, and I held my stare. He finally looked away, and I changed my focus to the bailiff who swore me in.

The prosecution went first, so Captain James asked me all the questions that we had gone over in his office. I answered all his questions honestly. He then told the judge that he had no further questions. That's when all hell broke loose. Johnson's attorney was a high-powered big-shot attorney that had been flown in from the United States. I found out that Johnson's father was a full-bird colonel in the army, which means that he was a very high-ranking officer. His father had a lot of money and influence. His dad actually outranked the entire jury. His attorney was a plump, semibald man with dark hair. He didn't dress well and looked like a pushover. That was until he spoke. He was the exact opposite of Captain James. He spoke with power, and when he talked, everyone listened. He fired into me like I was a target at a gun range. He tried to trip me up about everything that I remembered about the attack. He grilled me about my past as if I was the one who stabbed someone. I would look at Captain James to intervene, and he was just sitting there, looking confused. This man painted a picture of me to be larger than life. It was a picture of a "gangster," and his client was trying to defend himself against me. He brought in people that I was involved in altercations with. They testified that I was a very violent person. Captain James never intervened one time and let this guy eat my lunch.

When he was done, I felt like I was going to throw up. I felt like I was just led to the slaughter and left to fend for myself. I asked to go back to the hotel afterwards. I was so upset that I remained silent until I got into my hotel room. As soon as they closed the door to my room, I began to cry uncontrollably. I started throwing everything I could against the wall. I was so angry and devastated that this had just happened to me. I was emotionally, mentally, and spiritually drained. I cried until I fell asleep.

The next day, the jury went back for deliberation. I sat in a small room with Sean and Captain James. The first day ended without a verdict. We had to come back in the next day to see if they would make a ruling. We waited in silence for about five hours. At last, the bailiff came back and told us to make our way to the courtroom because the jury had reached a *decision*. We made our way into the packed courtroom where

I again saw Johnson sitting next to his high-powered attorney. His father was sitting behind him with his uniform on.

"Has the jury reached its verdict?" said the judge.

"Yes, Your Honor, we have," replied the head juror.

"You may proceed with the findings," the judge instructed.

"We find the defendant Private First Class Johnson not guilty of first-degree attempted murder," read the juror.

Gasps were heard throughout the courtroom. I was crushed at that moment. "I was sentenced to a life of pain while he gets off," I said to Captain James. He just shook his head.

The juror continued, "We, however, find the defendant guilty of aggravated assault with a deadly weapon and sentence him to two years in a federal penitentiary."

You have to be kidding me! Two years, two freaking years? I thought. I wanted to hop up out of my chair and strangle Johnson myself right there in the courtroom. "You mean to tell me that this man ruined my life, and he only gets two years?" I said. "This isn't justice." This was another critical point in my life. When that verdict was read, something died within me. Life seemed to be plotting against me. I thought that God obviously didn't care about me. I was angry, and I was devastated.

ESCAPE

When I got home from Germany, I was at another major crossroad in my life. I really had two choices: (1) I could deal with life positively, (2) I could deal with life negatively. Those are really the only two choices we ever have when we feel we have been harmed or wronged. In crisis, we can either choose to be victims or victors; there is no middle ground. Throughout life, we are going to be faced with tragedy and injustice. Unfortunately, there is no way around it.

I *decided* not to utilize any of the positive avenues of help that were at my disposal. I *decided* to bottle all of the rage and hurt inside of me. I became very bitter and enraged with God. I felt as though I was wronged. I felt demoralized, and I became empty inside. If there was a God, he didn't care about me, so in turn I didn't care about him. This left a void in my spirit. There is a place within all of us that is set aside for God. It can only be filled with him. When we move him out of our lives, there is no way we can feel whole. Once the void is there, we try to fill the void with other things. I did not know then how important a relationship with God was. Also, I had no clue how my *decisions* would impact not only my life but the lives of everyone around me.

The apartment we had in Silver Spring was sucking us dry, so we were forced to break our contract and move closer to my parents. We were forced to move into a low-income area. My wife was not happy at all about the downgrade in our living conditions. Our previous place was absolutely beautiful. It had a huge magnificent lobby when you walked in. Our apartment was on the seventh floor, so we had a spectacular view of the bustling downtown. My wife loved going to the little coffee shops and restaurants that were right outside the huge glass double doors of our building. Now we were in a rough run-down apartment complex. We were on the ground floor, so our bedroom window and sliding glass door were right off of the sidewalk. The inside was small, the carpets were old, and the appliances were ancient. We found out later that we had a serious roach problem as well. There were no fancy shops or stores around, and we had to drive everywhere. Luckily, our Honda Accord finally arrived from Germany, so at least we had transportation. There were always people hanging around outside at night, and my wife was scared to go anywhere after dark. The bad living conditions coupled with my horrible attitude strained our marriage to the breaking point.

Finally, she could take no more and left with my daughter. Again, I felt victimized by life. Now I couldn't even see my daughter. I was getting sick and tired of playing this game called life. I needed to *escape* from my thoughts. The only solace I could find was in alcohol. When I would drink, the pain would stop for a while. It started out with a couple beers at first to take the edge off. I quickly realized that alcohol took away all the things that were tormenting me. My foot would stop hurting, my mind would stop hurting, and my heart would stop hurting for a short time. I began drinking more and more as time went on. I just wanted to be numb. I did not want to think about my problems. Over time, I *decided* to make alcohol the number one priority in my life. I refused to talk about the pain with anyone. I wanted to seem like I was tough and that I could handle it. I didn't realize that I was making *decisions* that were impacting many lives. It was always "Poor me, look what happened to me." It felt like life was happening to me, and I had no control. What I didn't realize is that I always had a way out of the pain. God was waiting for me the whole time, gently tugging at me. I chose to ignore the tug by drinking myself into oblivion.

My apartment turned into the hangout spot for anyone who would bring over more alcohol. I tried to hide under the guise of wanting to party so people wouldn't know how bad I was hurting inside. I thought everyone just saw me having a good time and enjoying myself. Before I knew it, I was drinking almost every day. The only time I wouldn't drink was when I had a hangover and I was too sick to drink. My brother Arthur would come by often with his friends, and we would drink and play video games. It started out being cool for him because his older brother had a bachelor pad that he could come party at. At first I played it off well, I would laugh and joke with them as I chugged down beer after beer. Over time, however, Arthur started to notice that something wasn't right with me. I started getting very hostile and aggressive when I would get drunk. I would want to prove that just because I was hurt didn't mean that I was not the toughest dude in the room. I would try and "flex" on everyone that was around. I had the respect of them because of what I had made it through, but that respect was slowly dwindling.

"Arnold, you all right, man?" Arthur asked the day after I had been belligerently drunk.

"Why?" I said very hostile.

"Man, you are really drinking a lot," Arthur continued. "Are you sure everything is okay? You know you can talk to me."

"Everything is fine, man, I'm straight," I replied. "You know I can handle whatever comes my way, I'm good."

"It's just that you tried to fight me last night," said Arthur. "You know I would never hit you, but I almost had to last night. You are really getting worse, man, maybe you should try to slow down a little."

"Man, I said I'm good. I just drank too much last night," I retorted. "I will chill out with the liquor for a while and stick to the beer."

"All right, man, I love you and you know I'm here for you," Arthur said, concerned.

My younger brother is my best friend. I put him through hell growing up, but he has always looked up to me and been there for me. My stabbing affected him the most besides my mother. He even wrote a poem about what happened to me and how he felt during that time. The poem moved me to tears when I read it. I have always loved him as well even though I didn't show it as much as I should have. I really respected his word, so hearing him say those things really hurt me. I knew I was drinking too much, but I thought that it was my only *escape*. Again, I was given the opportunity to get some help, and I *decided* to turn it down. I *decided* to continue to *escape* from reality and not deal with the pain.

I was having more and more nightmares now. Night after night, I would go to sleep drunk and wake up in a panic drenched with sweat. The stabbing haunted me. I could feel the knife being driven into my body again and again. The hurt I felt mentally and physically became unbearable when I was sober. Alcohol became my medication, my therapist, and my god. For a couple of hours, I could be whom I wanted to be. It allowed me to step into a different reality. I worshipped it unknowingly. I used it to try and fill the massive void left open within me. I did not know that God reserved that place for himself. Any talk of God would irritate me and cause me to be defensive. I considered myself to be an atheist at this point, and I was proud of the label. I would agree with any teaching that talked about the nonexistence of God. I was completely spiritually bankrupt.

I started to become very paranoid about the fact that I was unable to protect myself fully. I moved into a very dangerous phase in my life, which put everyone around me at risk. I wanted to carry a gun on me at all times. I was able to purchase an old German .22 caliber handgun. It was the ugliest gun I had ever seen, but I made sure that people knew that I was now "strapped." I became obsessed with having a firearm on me. I imagined someone being able to overpower me now that I was injured, and I was not going to allow that to happen. If you saw me anywhere, rest assured that I was carrying a loaded illegal firearm. The scariest thing was that I would have used it if the right situation presented itself. I didn't care about anything or anyone at this point in time. I practiced pulling my gun out and cocking it as fast as I could in the mirror. I was prepared to shoot someone that tried to harm me. I had no problem going to prison for a "just" reason. I was a ticking time bomb.

I was still technically in the army at this point in time. I only had to call in once a week to my command. I never told the military about my deteriorating mental state. I *decided* to continue down my path of self-destruction despite the urging of family members and friends to get some help. I knew that by getting some help, I was going to have to face the demons that haunted me. I continued to *escape* with a bottle, it was so much easier. There was no way I wanted to sit in a room with a shrink, and pull all of these skeletons out of the closet. The thought of going through life sober terrified me. Alcohol was the best medicine in the world to me it was my only comfort. Losing that was not an option.

I stayed in my apartment for a full year in a blur. My lease was up, and so was my tenure in the army. I had very limited contact with my wife and daughter for almost six months now. I had no money coming in and nowhere to stay. I had to file for disability through the Veterans Administration because the army found my incident to be no fault of their own. There was no telling when I would start receiving checks for disability. I moved into my parents' basement, which slowed my drinking down but did not stop it. The problem was I had no money, so I had to find work. I found a job at a cell phone company where I would box up refurbished phones all day long. This was actually a bright spot in my life back then. I actually felt like I was moving forward a little bit. I had a reason to wake up in the morning, and I couldn't get plastered every night. I continued to drink but not nearly as heavy.

I started having conversations with my wife again over the phone. She wanted to be a family again, which really gave me a reason to try and straighten up. The only thing was that I still did not have a relationship with God, so every time I got upset, I had nothing to turn to but the bottle. I got rid of the gun and tried my best to straighten up on my own. What I now know is that I was doomed to fail again because I would not make the *decision* to reach out to God. He was tugging at me during this time, but I was still resentful and bitter deep down inside.

The day came when my wife decided to come back to the United States with my daughter. We all lived in my parents' basement together. It was tight quarters, but it was so great to see my daughter again. She was now a year old. Even though my wife and child were with me and my parents were upstairs, the addiction still had a stranglehold on me. I continued to get completely drunk and started being verbally abusive to my wife. I would wake up the next morning to see her crying and not remember what I did the night before. I tried going to AA meetings a couple of times to stop drinking, but I was never willing to deal with what happened to me. I wasn't willing to give up the anger I felt on the inside. I thought I was justified to carry the hatred and resentment towards Johnson, the justice system, and God. The sad thing was that I was destroying my family again and made the *decision* to not get help to stop it.

When I was sober, I tried to make everything right and tried to keep us together. But I was sober less and less as each day passed. I couldn't stop now on my own even if I wanted to. This problem was out of human hands; nothing anyone said or did could break this spell. Alcohol reigned supreme in my world. Only the power of God could restore me to sanity. It boggles my mind to think how insane a liquid can make an individual act. I was willing to destroy the lives of everyone around me just so I could stay inebriated. The worst part of all of was that the people I hurt the most were the ones who loved me the most. The woman who loved me and was willing to leave her family and come across the ocean for me stood no chance against the grip of alcoholism. She tried so hard to make it work for us but could not. She put up with many drunken nights with me breaking her down emotionally. When I was drunk, she was an easy target for me to attack because the next day, she would still love me. Deep down, I didn't want a family. I did not want to be responsible for anyone because I could not even take care of myself. I got tired of the guilt and shame I felt every morning after I got bombed the night before. I could not take having to wake up and have to see the hurt in her eyes. I couldn't take it anymore so I left.

I was so consumed by alcohol that I was willing to leave my family that had come from across the Earth to be with me. I was spiraling out of control. I couldn't control my emotions or my desire to drink. I moved into the basement of a friend from work. I slept on a mattress in a small damp and poorly lit room. The house was a disaster, but I didn't care because now I could be left alone to my pain and the only *escape* I knew.

DESPAIR

Why didn't I just die when I got stabbed? That question was on a constant loop in my mind. I didn't want to be here anymore; it hurt too badly. This game wasn't fair. There was no future for me. I felt that God had forsaken me and left me in the wilderness to perish alone. The rage and resentments were liquefying my insides. The past was all I could see. Sleep would not even give me peace; the nightmares robbed me of rest. I cared about no one, not even my firstborn child. *why didn't you let me die*! I would scream in a drunken rage. I was beyond any form of human restoration. I was in *despair*.

Drugs now became a very large part of my life. It took so much alcohol to get drunk now that I would become deathly ill the next day. Drugs accelerated the inebriation process, which lessened the hangover. Powder cocaine and ecstasy were now being consumed in massive quantities. I began selling drugs to allow myself unlimited access to them along with more financial ability to purchase. The lack of sleep led to further paranoia, which caused me to return to carrying firearms. The full-out destruction process had commenced.

My wife remained at my parents' house with my daughter for the next couple of months while I remained in my friend's basement. The house that was already a disaster had now turned into a drug house with my presence. Eventually, the house was raided by the police when I was on a drug run. Luckily, there were no drugs or weapons in the house when they came in, but they completely destroyed the entire house and left me with nowhere to go. Another friend of mine allowed me to stay with him in his empty room. There was no bed in the room, so I slept on the floor on top of blankets for cushion. I now had no contact with my wife and child. I didn't know where they were staying and didn't even care. I was an empty shell of a man, limping around this hell.

I received word that Tracy was granted an uncontested divorce. She was able to get a townhouse not far from me. I also heard that she had a new boyfriend who was stepping up to take the responsibilities that I had refused to take. Of course I used this as another excuse to put more drugs and alcohol into my body. I was now even scaring other drug buddies by the amounts of pure cocaine I would snort. I hoped maybe one of my binges would give me a heart attack to put me out of my misery. I developed a severe chronic cough, and I could finally feel my health start to slip away. That's what I really wanted to happen. I wanted to die every moment I was alive. I was just too scared to pull the trigger. I held my gun up to my head many nights with tears streaming down my face and could not bring myself to do it. I figured eventually the drugs and alcohol would do the dirty work for me.

On my twenty-fifth birthday, I finally *decided* to reach out for help. I was about fifteen beers into my thirty-pack, and I couldn't take it anymore. Deep down somewhere inside of me, I still wanted to live. I got on my cell phone and called 911. I told the operator that I needed an officer because I was going to kill myself or someone else if they did not come and pick me up. I walked out of the apartment and sat on the curb with my thirty-pack sitting beside me and waited for the police. They showed up and saw that I was completely broken. The female officer took me by the hand and gently sat me in the backseat.

My family came to visit me in the psychiatric emergency ward of the hospital where I was taken. When I saw my mother, I could no longer contain the hurt I felt inside and cried the deepest cry that I ever had in my life. The last three years of pain were finally being released from me. I thought that just maybe I had a shot to live again. A couple of days later, I was transferred to the psychiatric ward of the Veterans Hospital nearby. I spent two weeks there and was then transferred to a long-term treatment facility for veterans. While I was there, the doctors discovered that I was suffering from a severe case of untreated posttraumatic stress disorder. I also had depression as well as alcoholism and drug addiction.

This was the first time I had ever gotten brutally honest with how I felt and what was going on with me. My *decision* of not seeking treatment in the past almost took my life. I started to attend classes on all the conditions I suffered from where I learned a great deal about each of them. I learned different coping methods and strategies to deal with my feelings. I was doing much better for the first time in a long time. I was sober now for the longest I had been since I started drinking, and my thoughts were clearing up a little bit. I met a new woman and started having contact with my daughter again. Life seemed like it was on the up and up. I actually didn't want to die anymore.

Then one day, I was pulled into a conference room by my team of psychiatrists and doctors. They all had very solemn looks on their faces when I walked in.

"Arnold, we have some potentially bad news that we have to tell you," said the head doctor.

My heart immediately began to race. "Okay, is my family all right?" I said nervously.

"Your family is doing fine," the doctor continued. "We just received word that the man who stabbed you has appealed the ruling of the case. You are going to need to fly to Kentucky for a retrial in two weeks.

"What!" I exclaimed. "He wants a retrial for what? He only served two years for what he did to me."

"We do not know the details of the case," my psychiatrist said. "We just know that we need to try to prepare you mentally for this."

I was just getting my life back together, and life dropped another bomb on me. I was going to have to face this whole thing over again. I was going to have to look him in his eyes again. It shook me to my core. The last time we were in court, they basically turned me into a monster on the witness stand.

They blamed me for what happened to me. The rage started to boil up again inside. Fear gripped me again. I was right back into my old mental state in an instant. There was no one for me to cast my cares on. I still did not know God at this point. I needed a savior, but *decided* to go it alone again. I was still not willing to accept the fact that I needed God to get me through this. The heaviness was there again; the void opened up wide again. My spirit needed to be comforted.

I flew to Kentucky with my father to face Johnson again. I walked into the courtroom this time with a new level of hatred toward him. He not only stabbed me and left me partially paralyzed, he also ruined my entire life. I lost everything because of him. I did not take responsibility for my *decisions* at all. I was the victim; he was guilty for all of the anger, pain, and addiction in my life. I did not want to believe that I *decided* to handle what he had done to me the way I had. Yes, he was guilty of driving the knife into my body, but he didn't put the bottle to my mouth. He wasn't the one who denied and cursed God. That was my doing. I'm the one who handled my life that way.

My father made the trip with me to Kentucky. The new prosecutor filled me in on the trial when we got there. Apparently, there was some kind of technicality during the original case to warrant the appeal. He told me the bad news about us facing some serious challenges with the case. This was now four years after the stabbing took place, so many of the witnesses didn't make the trip from Germany. The ones that did make the trip forgot a lot of the details about the incident. There were many conflicting accounts of what took place that night. Also, the jury was not allowed to know that he had already been convicted and had served time for the crime. When we went to court the next day, the case completely fell apart. The whole experience was extremely hard to relive. We went over every gory detail once again. I had to sit on the witness stand and go through the same berating from the defense attorney. I stared Johnson down as many times as I could while I testified. I hated this man with every fiber of my being.

It was finally time for the verdict from the jury.

"We, the jury, find the defendant not guilty of all charges," read the head juror.

Johnson jumped up and hugged his family. I sat there stunned. This can't be right. I felt as though someone ripped my heart out of my chest. He was now going to have to be reimbursed for the two years he spent in the penitentiary. The United States government was now going to cut him a check for two years of active duty pay as a private first class. His record was now wiped completely clean. He could even join the military again if he wanted too. This was the final nail in the coffin.

Luckily, I received some great support from my therapists and doctors after the trial, or I would have exploded immediately. The support helped, but it wasn't enough. The anger set in so bad that I *decided* to buy a beer shortly after the case. This was the worst *decision* I could have made. The alcohol was like a friend I had not seen in a long while. It was so comforting to me. I slowly started sneaking off campus and began drinking again. There was that warm temporary escape again. I hid it well and graduated from the program. I *decided* that I was not going to go back to my hometown and found a place near the ocean. I got a little run-down apartment and set it up for my girlfriend to move in with me when she graduated treatment.

As soon as I got moved in, the drinking picked up again immediately. I was alone with my thoughts once more, which was not a safe place to be. Even though I was drinking again I managed to keep it somewhat together. Some of the techniques I learned in treatment helped me to deal with the memories most of the time. As long as the resentment lay dormant, I was okay. I could manage being alive until the anger showed its ugly head from inside its den.

My girlfriend finally graduated and moved in with me like we planned. We were moving forward slightly, and I now had the resemblance of a life. I was still drinking daily, but now I stayed in the house most of the time to stay out of trouble. We faced many problems in our relationship but the main one we faced was that we were two broken people. She had been through a lot in her life also. She was trying to put her life back together at the same time. Unknowingly we were in a relationship that was doomed to fail at some point.

We decided that we were going to use our GI Bill and go back to school. Together we enrolled in a local community college and began taking courses for our associates degrees. I chose to get my degree in computer networking while she chose to get hers in paralegal law. Even though I did not make it through high school and only had my GED, I was always fairly intelligent. Schoolwork always came very easily to me if I applied myself even a little. This was great for me at the time because it would allow us to make some pretty decent money and not have to work that hard for it. It also meant that I could continue to drink every night. We both got very good grades in school, which made it look like everything was going great. I would call home to update my parents of all the good marks I received, which made them happy and relieved to hear that I was doing better. They had no idea that every night, I was getting drunk.

A couple of months into living together, we found out my girlfriend was pregnant. I was very excited to have another shot at being a father. The major problem with that was that I was now completely back in the throes of alcoholism. I wanted to be a father so badly this time. I felt tremendous guilt and shame about how I quit on my oldest daughter. I tried so hard to make it seem like this time I was okay and could handle life finally. I was now becoming a hermit in hopes of not getting into any trouble. I would seclude myself in the apartment for days at a time. The only time I would go out would be to go to school and to the liquor store. I began to gain massive amounts of weight from lack of activity, beer, and overeating.

My pregnant girlfriend and I were now fighting every single day. It was such an unhealthy relationship, but because we were both so broken, we stayed together. I asked her to marry me so she wouldn't leave me, and she reluctantly said yes. We went down to the courthouse where we were married with no witnesses. I was determined to see this child even if it took marriage again. I was willing to do anything as long as I did not have to quit drinking. Throughout all the *despair* we faced together, neither she nor I would even entertain the God conversation. It seemed that God had wronged us both in irreconcilable ways. The void set aside for God was a gaping hole within both of us.

We somehow managed to not kill each other before the baby was born. Some months later, another healthy beautiful girl came into the world. I was in tears watching the delivery. *I could try and do it right this time,* I thought to myself. *I could bond with her from the beginning and be a father again.* She was and is my little angel. Of course when we got home, I celebrated by getting drunk. I did my best to slow down at first but to no avail. I spent most of my time in the house eating and drinking while she was an infant. I went to school and made sure most of the bills were paid. In my heart, I wanted to do right by her so badly it hurt. When I would end up getting drunk, I would wake up with such a feeling of guilt and shame. I just could not get straight no matter what I tried. The guilt coupled with the deep-rooted resentment led me back down the path of depression and despair.

Time passed, and I was now missing school, sleeping all day, and drinking all night long. Alcoholism is such a progressive disease; once it has you, it traps you in a vicious cycle of destruction. Life seemed like it was repeating itself all over again. I was slowly destroying another family with alcohol and depression. I now weighed in at 280 pounds and had problems moving around. I watched around eight to ten hours of TV a day with the shades drawn. My new wife and baby were left to fend for themselves in the apartment because I was incapacitated.

"You failed again Arnold," said the voice within. "You thought you were going to get your life together, and you failed again. You're a loser, your fat, you're a drunk. You might as well die because you'll never be able to change."

That is what I heard inside all day every day until I would get drunk again. Why should I even try to change? I gave it everything I had already and fell flat on my face again. I believed that I was doomed to a horrible alcoholic death. I failed my new baby daughter the way I had failed my first little angel. There was no reason to go on like this.

December 31, 2010, I broke down while I was chugging vodka straight out of the bottle. "God, if you exist, please have mercy on me and let me die or help me. If you won't let me die, then HELP ME PLEASE! PLEASE HELP ME!"

That was the prayer I said before I blacked out. I had finally surrendered my will. I was finally broken to the point of no return. I couldn't kill myself, so my only other option was to cry out to a God that I didn't know even existed. I did not know it then, but that prayer saved my life and began a process of healing from within.

REBIRTH

New Year's Day 2011, I woke up in a haze. I had no memory of anything that happened past the early evening of the day before. *Did I see the ball drop?* I thought. I sat on the edge of the bed trying to dig deep for any memories of the New Year's celebration to no avail. I made my way out to the living room where I saw my wife holding our little girl. She did not acknowledge the fact that I had entered the room.

"Happy New Year, baby," I said.

She turned to face me and I saw a look I had never seen on her face before. She looked like a woman who was tired of hurting inside and could not take it anymore.

"I can't do this, Arnold," she said with a very cold tone. "I am done with this. I am taking the baby and moving in with my brother."

We had been through a lot during our relationship, but I never heard her say that she was leaving. The tone of her voice told me that this was not an empty threat. She was really going to leave me.

"Why? What happened?" I stammered.

"You don't remember what you did last night again?" she questioned.

I looked down and shook my head no. My heart started pounding as the nervousness reached its pinnacle. *What had I done this time?* I asked myself. It is the worst feeling in the world to have someone that you love being hurt by you and you cannot even remember what you did. It was so scary to think that I could actually kill someone and never remember doing it.

"You were sloppy drunk again like always," she barked. "You were cussing me out in front of the neighbors. You kept telling me that you hated me and that you never loved me. You really hurt me last night, Arnold. I am done with you and your drinking. You are getting worse. I am scared to see what is going to happen down the road."

The fear of not seeing my little girl again terrified me. I could not go on if I lost another child to alcohol. In that very instant, I made a *decision* that would change my life forever. I *decided* deep down in the core of my being that I was going to do whatever it took to stop drinking. I did not remember at that point that I had cried out to God for help the night before. He finally was allowed to step in and stop the destruction. I have found out that God is a gentleman and he will not come in when he is not welcome. I believe that God gave me the strength to make a true *decision* to change.

"I am going to quit, baby," I pleaded. "I will get some help this time, I swear."

My wife had seen my many weak attempts to quit that never lasted more than a week. She was not really impressed with my promise whatsoever. She just looked away.

"I am so sorry for all of the wrong I have done to you," I said as I sat down beside her. "Baby, please give me one more shot. If I drink again, I will help you pack your things. I am so serious. I will not lose another family. I will do whatever it takes to stay sober this time."

"This is your last chance, Arnold," she reluctantly said. "I swear if I see you drink again, we are leaving."

I had one last shot to get myself straight. There was a completely new feeling this time. I felt like I could do it. The rest of that day, I lay on the couch to recover from the horrible hangover I had. While lying there, I was formulating a plan to get sober in my head. I knew from experience that there was no way I was going to stop on my own. I could not risk it. There was no room for error in this situation. I *decided* that I was going to contact the Veterans Administration in the morning.

The next morning, I woke up early and was very anxious to make my call for help. This was the first time I was actually excited about the possibility of being free from alcohol. I called the main number to the hospital to find out who I needed to speak with. The operator answered and asked whom I would like to speak to. I told her that I needed to speak to someone about alcoholism. She transferred me to another department and they asked the same question. I answered the same way and was transferred to another department again. A lot of people were off work because of the holiday, and I ended up being transferred three more times. Finally, I got a hold of a gentleman who told me that I had to come in and speak to someone in person. I immediately rushed off to get dressed and ready to go.

Once I arrived at the office, I met with a nice gentleman that asked me a lot of questions. I answered them all honestly. He told me I had to go to the main hospital to meet with a lady who was in charge of the substance abuse program. I needed to hurry because the hospital was twenty-five miles away, and she was only working a half day. I sped off to the hospital with a sense of accomplishment. All these hoops I had to jump through would have frustrated me before, and I would have put the entire thing off. This time was different. I would have driven anywhere in the country. I got to her office just as she was packing up for the day. I told her that I needed help and was willing to do whatever it took to get it. She could see the determination and desire for a change in my eyes. This nice lady made some calls and pulled some strings to get me into an outpatient program the next day. I would have to leave my house every morning at seven, and drive thirty miles to take part in the program. I did not care about any of that. I gave her a big hug before I left her office. I was so grateful.

I completely immersed myself into the program. I attended every class, read all the material, and participated fully. There was a driving force that was so mysterious to me at the time. I could not slow down or stop. Some of the people at the treatment program told me that I may want to pace myself because this was a marathon and not a sprint. I told them that I could not contain it; there was a fire burning deep inside of me. I know now that God took over to get me where he wanted me to be. He needed to do a lot of work in me before he could use me.

Life started to take on a new dimension. The beauty of life began to appear to me. I would go to the ocean before sunrise and watch the sun come up on the horizon. During the day, I would find myself staring up at the sky in amazement of the beauty. For so long, life was painful and hard, I never saw the beauty of creation. My home life began to improve dramatically. My wife and I weren't arguing nearly as much. I was even helping around the house. The experience of being a father became almost magical. I would spend hours playing with my daughter. Her laugh was the best sound in the world to me. I was alive for the first time since I could remember.

I stayed at the program until I completely outgrew it. I was now forty-five days sober. The majority of people that were in the program with me were forced to be there by family members or the judicial system. Most of them had no desire to stay sober, and they would talk about how they were going to get drunk once they were done. I told my counselors that I felt like I needed to move on with my recovery. They all agreed. I started attending three to four AA meetings a day. AA was my comfort zone because the people there were interested in what I was interested in, which was staying sober. I met so many great people that had been through their own hell and made it out. They could identify with the pain and the hopelessness. I got a sponsor who started taking me through the twelve steps. My sponsor had over twenty-five years of sobriety. He was a powerful man that commanded respect. When he spoke, people would listen. I wanted what he had. I wanted to be like him. My sponsor ran a men's workshop that I attended every Saturday morning. He started to show me what was possible if I stayed straight.

I made it through my first step of the AA program, which dealt with admitting that I could never drink again responsibly. We moved on to step two, which I was not very excited about because this step involved believing in God. Even though my life was now becoming amazing, there were still deep-rooted negative feelings towards God. However, I could not deny what I was seeing in so many other people. Some of these people had been through worse things than me. Many of them destroyed their lives way more than I had. Some of them had literally crawled out of the gutter. They would come to the meetings every day smiling and happy. They were now productive members of society, and you would never know what they had been through if they did not tell you. Each and every one of them gave all the credit to God for their transformations. They made a very strong case for the Creator. I was willing at this point to at least try to make contact with him again.

Once I opened the door for God, my life completely changed forever. Now he could work on a willing participant. Shortly after I made the *decision* to make contact with him, he revealed himself to me. I was lying on my bed reading a book when I felt the presence of someone else in the room with me. I put the book down and looked up, but there was no one there. In that instant, the light from the lamp behind me softened. I was transported in my mind to the time when I was lying on the frozen asphalt bleeding to death. God was reminding me of the moment all the pain was taken away, and the panic stopped. I felt the overwhelming feeling of love that I experienced that night. I remembered how the presence of God engulfed me and held me ever so gently. The feeling lasted for only a short time before I heard a voice inside of me.

"Arnold, my son," said the voice. "I love you and have always loved you. I have been here all along waiting for you to come to me. I have kept you while you struggled your way through life without me. I have plans for your life, but you need to remain with me."

That was a transformational moment in my life because at that moment I knew God was real. I had completely forgotten about that experience eight years before. All I could remember about the stabbing was the terror and the pain. I had suppressed the memory of my experience with God. He made certain that I not only remembered it but felt it as well. He spoke so clearly to me that night. God made sure there was no way I could deny him after that. I now knew that he loved me and cared about me as an individual. This began my first ever true walk with God.

The void that I had always been trying to fill in my soul was now beginning to fill up. Life felt different now. There was a sense of purpose for the first time. I knew that I was on this planet for a reason. For so long, I believed that life meant nothing and went nowhere. I still did not know anything about him, but just the fact that I knew he existed meant everything. I told anyone who would listen about what had happened to me. My parents were so relieved to hear me acknowledge God. They are both very devout Christians who tried desperately to get me to open my eyes and accept God in my life. They came at me with the Bible and Jesus, and I just could not understand how they believed in that book of fairy tales. I thought people who believed in that were uneducated and gullible. God knew all of this of course, so he came to me in a way that I could accept at first.

As my new life with God went on, I started to pray constantly. I started step three in AA, which is where you turn your will and your life over to the care of God. I prayed many times a day for his will to be done and not mine. The more I prayed that prayer, the more I saw images of Jesus Christ. Everywhere I turned, I saw Jesus's face. I saw him on TV commercials, flyers, and bumper stickers. I now started to notice all the churches in my area. I would read messages like "Jesus is waiting for you" and "Jesus loves you" on church marquees. For two years I had driven by the same church in my neighborhood and barely noticed it. Now I was being drawn to it. I could not fight it anymore. It was getting to be overwhelming. One Wednesday afternoon, I was lying on the couch and flipping through the channels and stopped on a channel that was playing *The Passion of the Christ*. I caught it at the end when Jesus was on the cross, and he said, "Forgive them, Father, for they know not what they've done." That was a very emotional moment for me. I *decided* that I was going to go to the church in my neighborhood that night. I saw a sign in front of the church earlier that day that said they had a Wednesday evening service.

I timidly walked in the church. It was already completely full when I got there. There was a band up in front playing Christian music very loud. There were many people in the crowd with their hands up in the air, singing along with the band. I almost turned around and walked out, but I was now being led in by the hand of God. I took a seat in the back of the church and tried to not be as nervous as I was. Directly in the middle of the stage was a lone microphone on its stand. All of a sudden, a young woman walked up and approached the microphone. The music went way down, almost to the point of not being audible. The young lady stepped up to the microphone and adjusted it to her height. She began to tell a story of a horrible accident that she had been in. She briefly described the scene while in tears. At the end of her description of the horrendous scene, she broke down sobbing. A man came up and put his arm around her as she continued. She then described a feeling just like the one I felt the night that I was stabbed. I broke down crying in that moment. Someone else had felt the same feeling I had. As I cried, she continued to tell the congregation how Jesus was that feeling, and how he had saved her life.

The man who had his arm around her took the microphone as she walked off the stage. He said that he was the pastor of the church and that this was testimony night. He said if anyone had a testimony of how God had saved them or helped them through something, they could come up and tell the church. I immediately heard that voice within tell me that I needed to get up and tell my testimony. I was like "You want me to do what? This is my first time here, and I do not know anyone." The voice became increasingly louder as I procrastinated. There was such a strong tug on me to go up there that I had no choice but to get up and do it.

I slowly walked my way up to the stage, and the music went down again. I started to sweat and breathe very hard. I thought I was going to pass out from fear. I made it to the microphone and started to speak.

"My...my n-name is...Arnold. A-and this...is my f-first time...here," I stuttered "I do not know much about God, but I know he is real. He has saved my life."

I told them a brief-three minute synopsis of the events during the last eight years. I was honest about my alcoholism and depression. Once I was done, I saw several people crying in the audience. Everyone stood up and clapped for me. I knew at that moment that Jesus was real. I also knew that everything I had gone through was not in vain, that all the pain could now be used for good somehow.

RENEWED

Following the experience at the church, I began attending every service that they had. I got to know the pastor, and we had many long talks about Jesus Christ. I was baptized in water within two weeks. I was now reborn, and I became so hungry for more knowledge of God. I read the Bible daily along with any book that would help my relationship with Christ. I fasted for days to get closer to him. There was a peace over me that I had never experienced before. The glory and majesty of Jesus was being revealed to me each moment. The void was gone.

As time went on, I drew closer and closer to God. I envisioned everything being perfect from there on out. What I did not know was that being saved did not mean that I was immune to trials and tribulation in my life. Out of nowhere, many challenges began taking place. Although it started to get hard, I now had someone to rely on for support. It was great to be able to cast my cares on God when I went through the struggles. I prayed and prayed but felt at times that I was being tested. Turmoil started to pop up with my wife, and financial issues started to arise. I could not understand why these things were happening. I started to get really stressed out. It did not make sense to me why all these things started to happen at the same time. I was saved now, wasn't life supposed to immediately get better? It was becoming obvious that my hopes of a perfect life were not going to come to pass. The problems were now starting to get worse and worse. My faith was really starting to waver, and I started to back off from God. I was praying less, and reading my Bible less. Frustration set in, and instead of *deciding* to lean more on Jesus, I tried to work things out on my own.

Eventually, I came to the breaking point and wanted to go back to my old life again. This new God thing was not working. Problems at home were getting so bad that my wife finally left to go stay with her family for a "break." About a week later, she called me and told me that she found out that she was pregnant. We were both shocked by the news. "What next, Father?" I asked. "How are we going to raise another baby together while we are fighting the way we are?" After I got off the phone with her, I *decided* to take the three-hour drive to see her and my daughter. I kept thinking, *How on Earth did everything just take a turn for the worst like this?* I did not drink, but the thought started to cross my mind more and more. The enemy now had an opening, and he was throwing everything he had at me.

"This is not working, why don't you just go back to your old life?" said a voice within. "You gave it your best shot, and everything started to get worse. Look, your wife left with the baby, where was God when you needed him?" The voice grew louder and louder and really started to convince me. I needed to get out of my head. I still had not picked up a drink, but the desire was so strong.

During the drive, I was very depressed, and I was so close to *deciding* to just go back to the old me. Then my phone rang. I was not going to answer it because I was too upset and did not even recognize the number. However, something inside told me to pick up the phone.

"Hello," I said.

The person on the other line said. "Hey, Arnold, I do not know if you remember me, but you helped me a couple of weeks ago when I was going through some tough times in my life. My name is James."

I thought for a second trying to remember him. Then an image of his faced popped in my mind. He and I talked one day after an AA meeting about Christ. He needed some help because he was struggling with trying not to drink. And I gave him a word of encouragement. "Yeah, I remember you, James, how you been?" I said.

"Look, Arnold, this is going to sound crazy," James continued. "You believe in God, right?"

I said, "Yes, you know I do."

James's voice quickened. "I have been able to hear directly from him ever since I was a young child. Today, he has been telling me that I needed to call you. I tried not to do it all day, but his voice just kept getting louder and louder."

I was completely silent while he spoke.

He continued, "Well, God told me to tell you this so that you know that it is him. He says that you are going through a tough time in your life right now. He also told me that your wife is pregnant, and your relationship is struggling."

We had not told anyone about her being pregnant. It had to be God.

James kept talking. "He told me to tell you that he loves you, Arnold. He says that he has huge plans for your life, but you need to be strong."

I started crying. As I looked ahead of me; the sky was absolutely gorgeous. The sun was going down so the clouds were the most beautiful I had ever seen them. They were a magnificent pink and purple with a deep orange coming from behind them. While I stared at the sky, the conversation switched. James voice was talking to me, but it was not him speaking. God started speaking directly to me through him.

God said, "I love you, my son. I need you to be strong right now, Arnold. You are at a major crossroads again in your life. I need you to make the right *decision* now. I have a plan and a purpose for you. It is your choice which way you go from here on out. Choose wisely."

James and I sat there in silence for at least two minutes. Had we just heard God speak?

Finally, James spoke. "That has never happened to me before. That was not me, Arnold."

"I know," I whispered. "That was God."

I thanked James for making the call, and we hung up the phone. I had to pull over to take in what had just happened. I looked up to the sky and thanked him for loving me enough to speak to me directly. I *decided* at that point that no matter what the situation, I was going to have faith in Jesus Christ. I learned a lot from that situation. I learned that sometimes we have to go through struggle in our walk with God to be taken to the next level. Sometimes we have to be broken down to remember that he is Lord. I learned that no matter what came my way, I needed to rely on him to carry me through.

I met with my wife and told her what happened. We talked for a long while, and she decided to come back home with me. When I got home, I found out why I went through the test that I had just experienced. God was getting ready to take me to the next level in my life. He wanted to make sure that when I started to go up the ladder of success, that I will continue to keep my eyes on him and him alone. About two weeks after my experience with God, I made a very heartfelt prayer to him. I wanted an opportunity to grow more. I prayed for him to give me something that I could sink my teeth into.

The next day after the prayer, I went to a church picnic. I ate and talked for a little while and *decided* to leave. As I was walking down the hill, a man named Steve was coming towards me. Steve and I had talked a few times but always very briefly. From our previous conversations, I knew he owned a very large contracting company in the area. As we passed each other, he stopped me and said that God put something on his heart that he needed to show me. I knew he was a nice guy and that he was very successful in business, so I agreed to meet with him. The next day, we met at a local coffee shop and talked. He told me that there was a business expanding in the area, and there was an opportunity for me to be involved. I was blown away. *I just prayed for this!* I thought to myself. He showed me a video of the business, and it made perfect sense to me. I was in! The only problem was that it cost $500 to join, which I did not have. Even though I did not have the full amount, I told him that I would be in tomorrow. I went to my house that evening and thought about how to get the money. I knew that this was God working in my life, so I was open to anything. As I sat in my apartment, I got the idea to sell my PlayStation3 and all my video games for the money. I had absolute faith that this is exactly what I prayed for, so I packed it all up and took everything to the pawnshop. When they gave me a quote for how much it was worth, I was amazed that it was exactly how much I needed to get in.

The next day, I called Steve back and told him I was ready to get started. A couple of hours later, he came over with the contract. I filled everything out and was now a business owner. There was another problem though, which was I did not know what to do from that point. God had me covered for that. He had Steve take me under his wing. Steve showed me how to think like a professional, dress like a professional, and act like a professional. He and I spent many hours together talking about business as well as how to grow stronger in my faith. About a month into the business, I was told that there was going to be a conference in California that I needed to attend. Steve told me that this was where all of the top people were going to teach me everything about the business.

I thought that there was no way I was going to be able to make it. I had just pawned my video games to get in, and now they want me to buy a plane ticket to California? I thought he was crazy. He told me that if I really wanted to do this business right, then I had to go. I thought about it for a little while, and *decided* that I was going to go no matter what. I again went into my house and asked God how I was going to come up with the money. He told me to get rid of the stuff I no longer needed. I *decided* to sell everything I did not use. I sold a flat screen TV, a juicer, a grill, and a coffee maker. My wife thought I was absolutely crazy by this time. I told her that God is working in my life right now and I have to do it. Every dollar that I received from the items I sold I put in a jar that had a label on the front that read "California or bust!"

I raised the money for the ticket, so Steve told me that he would let me stay in his hotel room. Before I knew it, I was in California wearing a suit with thousands of other business people. I was so amazed that life had changed so drastically that quickly. The business conference really changed the belief level I had in myself and my own capabilities. I heard testimonies of people that came from nothing and completely changed their lives. They told me that if I started to develop and refine myself, I could do anything and have anything I wanted in life. I was now determined to make this work at all costs. Soon Steve and I returned home. He and I got straight to work and built a substantial business in our area. I was waking up early every morning putting on a suit and finally holding my head high. I felt like I was becoming a new man.

God had given me a second chance at life. I turned off the TV completely and stuck my head into books. I read ravenously; I wanted to grow and learn as much as possible. I attended every conference and business meeting there was. I was 100 percent committed to personal growth and development. My walk with God strengthened while I grew as a businessman. The desire to drink was completely removed from me. The person that God had created me to be began to surface. I did not even recognize myself in the mirror. All my old friends were cut completely off. If you weren't growing and developing yourself, then we could not be friends. Things still were not perfect at home, but I was trying to be a better father and husband.

Eventually, my wife and I decided to move closer to family so we could have help with the new baby. Steve connected me with some business people in that area, and I continued building the organization. My wife and I stayed with my parents for a while, which was a very difficult situation. I'll be the first to admit that I made some bad *decisions* during the time we stayed with family, but I kept my faith in God. We found a condominium that was close by my parents' house and moved in. The move had no effect on the stress and strain that continued in our marriage. I was growing and developing in leaps and bounds, and I was just not the same person she met at the treatment center. I was now focused, driven, and very spiritual. Shortly after, we had my third beautiful little daughter, but we both could take it no longer and ended up separating.

It really turned out to be the best thing that could have happened to us. Sometimes, God has to shut some of the doors we opened in our past to move us forward. After the separation, I took on the role of a single father to my middle child while my wife kept the baby. It has been difficult at times to raise a little girl while trying to grow and build a business, but God has kept us. I have also regained contact with my oldest daughter. My ex-wife and I are not at odds about the separation, and we each have contact with the two girls. I thank God every day for the opportunity to be a father to my little princesses. I have regained my health and lost almost one hundred pounds. I am now a motivational speaker, and I get the honor of helping play a role in changing people's lives. The desire to use drugs and alcohol has been completely removed from my life. I have forgiven the man who stabbed me, and I pray for him till this day. I am now a positive role model in my family as well as in the community. Christ has *renewed* my mind, spirit, and body through his grace, mercy, and love.

In closing, I want to speak to the person who still suffers. There is a new life waiting for you. No matter what you have been through in life or how far down the scale you have gone, there is hope. The good news is that there are always positive ways to deal with the hurt. We have a God who loves us and will take away the pain if we ask. We have family that we can talk to. We also have doctors and therapists that will listen. God loves you and cares for you as an individual. Sometimes bad things happen that we cannot explain. I know how it feels to not have hope and feel like you are drowning under life's problems. I pray that my testimony of God's love and mercy will inspire you to reach out to him. If I can help one person experience the peace and love of Christ that I have felt, then everything I went through was not in vain. All that God needs is for you to crack the door of your heart a little bit for him to begin working in your life. The fact that you are still alive means there is a purpose and a plan for your life. Do not quit, do not stop fighting. You are more than a conqueror. You can be completely restored because Jesus Christ is real, and he is waiting for you.